THE MESSAGE OF MEDJUGORJE

The Marian Message to the Modern World

Mark I. Miravalle, S.T.D.

D1556949

UNIVERSITY
PRESS OF
AMERICA

LANHAM • NEW YORK • LONDON

Copyright © 1986 by

University Press of America,® Inc.

4720 Boston Way
Lanham, MD 20706

3 Henrietta Street
London WC2E 8LU England

Library of Congress Cataloging in Publication Data

Miravalle, Mark I., 1959-
   The message of Medjugorje.

   Adaptation of thesis (doctoral)—Pontifical
University of St. Thomas Aquinas (Angelicum), Rome.
   Bibliography: p.
   1. Mary, Blessed Virgin, Saint—Apparitions and
miracles—Yugoslavia—Medugorje (Bosnia and Hercegovina)
2. Catholic Church—Doctrines.   3. Medugorje (Bosnia
and Hercegovina)—Religious life and customs.
I. Title.
BT660.M44M57   1986   232.91'7'0949742   86-1588
ISBN 0-8191-5288-9 (alk. paper)
ISBN 0-8191-5289-7 (pbk. : alk. paper)

All University Press of America books are produced on acid-free
paper which exceeds the minimum standards set by the National
Historical Publications and Records Commission.

DEDICATION

To St. Joseph and his Family,
and to Beth and our family.

ACKNOWLEDGEMENTS

The author wishes to bestow his heartfelt thanks to the following individuals for their invaluable assistance in the completion of this work:

— to Sr. Lucy Rooney, S.N.D. and Fr. Robert Faricy, S.J., from the Gregorianum in Rome;

— to Fr. Jordan Aumann, O.P., and Fr. Giles Dimock, O.P. from the Angelicum in Rome;

— to Fr. Svetozar Kraljevic, O.F.M., and Miss Anita Curtis from the community at Medjugorje;

— to Fr. Gerard McGinnity, Senior Dean at the Irish National Seminary, Ireland;

— to Mr. and Mrs. John Smalley for their generous support of this work;

— to Mr. Michael Mollerus and Miss Darlene Lawless for their efforts in the technical preparation of this work;

— to the Word Among Us Press for permission to quote from the text of René Laurentin and Ljudevit Rupcic, *Is the Virgin Mary Appearing at Medjugorje?*, Washington, D.C., 1984;

— and to all family and friends whose prayers and support made this work possible.

DECLARATION

The decree of the Congregation for the Propagation of the Faith, A.A.S. 58, 1186 (approved by Pope Paul VI on October 14, 1966) states that the *Nihil Obstat* and *Imprimatur* are no longer required on publications that deal with private revelations, provided that the text contains nothing contrary to faith and morals.

This book represents an adaption of a doctoral dissertation successfully defended at the Pontifical University of St. Thomas Aquinas (Angelicum) in Rome, the thesis of which sought to illustrate theologically that the "Message" of Medjugorje represents an authentic embodiment of sound Catholic doctrine as dictated by the Church's Magisterium. The dissertation received the pontifical university's *Vidimus et Approbavimus* as a work free from any doctrinal statement contrary to faith and morals.

TABLE OF CONTENTS

Preface to Third Printing   xiii
Introduction   xv
Chapter One: *The Content of the*
Message of Medjugorje   1
    Messages of the First Seven Days,
       June 24 to June 30, 1981   3
    Messages from July, 1981 to December, 1983   6
    Messages from July, 1981 to December, 1983
       Without Specific Chronological Data   8
    Interview with Mirjana Dragicevic
       January 10, 1983   10
    Account of the Message of Medjugorje
       Sent to Pope John Paul II by
       Fr. Tomislav Vlasic and the
       Visionaries, November 30, 1983   21
    Messages through Jelena Vasilj,
       "The Seventh Visionary"   24
    Thursday Messages to the Parish
       March, 1984 to March, 1985   31
    Messages Reported Between June, 1984
       and December, 1984 Without Specific
       Chronological Data   39

Chapter Two: *Doctrinal and Thematic*
Synthesis of the Medjugorje Message   45
    A. Medjugorje Foundational Themes   45
       1. Faith   45
       2. Prayer   46
       3. Fasting   47
       4. Penance   47
       5. Conversion   47
       6. Peace   48
    B. Medjugorje Developmental Themes   49
       1. Jesus Christ—The One Redeemer
          and Mediator   49
       2. Renewal in the Holy Spirit   50

3. *Mary—Universal Mother and Intercessor*   50
4. *Mass and Eucharastic Adoration*   51
5. *Sacramental Confession*   52
6. *The Rosary*   52
7. *Renewal of Sacred Scripture*   53
8. *Devotion to the Sacred Heart of
   Jesus and the Immaculate Heart
   of Mary*   53
9. *Heaven, Purgatory, Hell, and Satan*   54
9. *Heaven, Purgatory, Hell, and Satan*   54
10. *Ecumenism*   55
11. *Family and Community Prayer*   56
12. *Offering of Suffering and Sacrifice*   56
13. *Abandonment to God*   57
14. *Eschatalogical Urgency*   58
Summary Statement   59

Chapter III: *Presence of the Medjugorje
Foundational Content in the Gospels
and the Apostolic Fathers*   63
Faith   63
1. *Faith in the Gospels*   63
2. *Faith in the Apostolic Fathers*   65
Prayer   66
1. *Prayer in the Gospels*   66
2. *Prayer in the Apostolic Fathers*   67
Fasting   68
1. *Fasting in the Gospels*   68
2. *Fasting in the Apostolic Fathers*   69
Penance   69
1. *Penance in the Gospels*   69
2. *Penance in the Apostolic Fathers*   70
Conversion   70
1. *Conversion in the Gospels*   70
2. *Conversion to the Apostolic Fathers*   72
Peace   73
1. *Peace in the Gospels*   73
2. *Peace in the Apostolic Fathers*   75
Summary Statement   76

Chapter Four: *Presence of the Medjugorje
Developmental Content in the Documents of
Vatican Council II and Post-Conciliar Documents*   79
Jesus Christ—The One Redeemer and Mediator   79

Renewal in the Holy Spirit   81
Mary—Universal Mother and Intercessor   83
Mass and Eucharastic Adoration   85
Sacramental Confession   86
The Rosary   87
Renewal of Sacred Scripture   88
Devotion to the Sacred Heart of Jesus
   and the Immaculate Heart of Mary   89
Heaven, Purgatory, Hell, and Satan   92
Ecumenism   93
Family and Community Prayer   95
Offering of Sufferings and Sacrifices   96
Abandonment to God   97
Eschatological Urgency   98
Summary Statement   100

Chapter Five: *The Message of Medjugorje in*
Relation to the Messages of Lourdes and Fatima   103
The Message of Lourdes   104
The Message of Fatima   109
Medjugorje: A Continuation of Fatima and Lourdes   121
Medjugorje: New Elements in the Marian Message   126
Summary Statement   127

Conclusion   131

Appendix I: *Revealed Prayers from*
Fatima and Medjugorje   133

Appendix II: *Medjugorjian Message Update*   139

Bibliography   153

PREFACE TO THIRD PRINTING

One aspect of the Message of Medjugorje that will not appear in the following pages is a pastoral note concerning the message offered to me by Marija Pavlovic, one of the young visionaries reported to see the "Gospa", the Blessed Virgin Mary on a daily basis since June, 1981.

During a conversation with Marija in our mutually substandard grasp of Italian, she confirmed two elements regarding the Madonna's words that place the Medjugorjian message in both its global and its personal perspective.

Firstly, Marija stated that the message of Medjugorje is a Marian message intended not only for the people of St. James Parish, nor just for the region and its surroundings, but comprises a Marian message for the *entire world*. Marija reported a message conveyed by the Madonna that stated: "The world is my parish, but there are many hearts not open to my words." Clearly then, the message of Medjugorje must unmistakenly be considered a global message for anyone, in the reported words of the Blessed Mother, with an "open heart."

Secondly, Marija confirmed that the contents of the message of the "Queen of Peace" must remain objective, without alteration or change; but that it should be personally incorporated as *gradually* as is personally necessary.

Marija used herself as an example in the need to incorporate gradually the sometimes challenging calls of Christian prayer and penance contained in the message. She said that when the Madonna began by asking for a daily prayer consisting of seven Our Father's, Hail Mary's, Glory Be's, and the Creed, Marija wondered how she would be able to fit this much prayer into each day. Marija had the same initial response to the Madonna's call for the daily Rosary, and again when that developed into the call for the full fifteen decade Rosary daily. But as the increases in the call to prayer came gradually, over a five year period of time, and Marija faithfully answered each call of this period, she summarized the fruits of her perseverance by saying to me, "And now, I want to pray always." The young visionary is attesting to the basic principle of the spiritual life which speaks of the gradual need for perseverance and faithfulness in becoming more generous in one's answer to the Christian call to prayer and penance, the fruits of which will allow for a consistent level of prayer and sacrifice far above the individual's previous expectations.

The need to safeguard the objectivity of the message reported by the visionaries is likewise of crucial importance. Oftentimes, there is the temptation to take the actual directives of any public or private revelation originated by God, and to reduce them to the degree that the individual conveying the message thinks is appropriate. To the extent that this takes place, the message ceases to be a divinely revealed message and instead becomes the message of the human conveyor, which defeats the essential purpose of a divinely ordained revelation. Hence Marija strongly confirmed the imperative to convey the reported Medjugorje message *in its fullness*, regardless of each individual's ability to incorporate personally the message in its fullness. The personal incorporation of any Marian message presupposes the use of Christian prudence (coupled with generous devotion) on the part of the faithful, taking into account personal factors, such as age, health, and one's state in life.

Perhaps Marija's pastoral notes concerning both the objective promulgation and the personal incorporation of the message of Medjugorje are best summarized in this June 9, 1984 message from the Queen of Peace to the parish of St. James, as reported by the visionaries:

> Dear children! Pray for the Spirit of Truth. . . . You need the Spirit of Truth in order to be able to convey the messages the way they are, without adding to them, or taking away anything: the way I gave them to you. Pray that the Holy Spirit may inspire you with the spirit of prayer, that you may pray more. I, as your Mother, say you pray little. Thank you for your response to my call.

INTRODUCTION

Before discussing the focus of this study, it is crucial for an accurate understanding of this examination that the following clarifications be made.

Firstly, this study is a theological analysis of the content of the messages attributed to the Blessed Virgin Mary by seven Croatian youths in a small Yugoslavian village known as Medjugorje. This study makes no explicit judgment as to the supernatural character of the apparitions, a judgment officially made only by the teaching authority of the Catholic Church (Magisterium). Hence, what is to follow will be an examination of their contents in the light of recognized sources of Christian truth and faith.

Secondly, because this study concerns only the content of the messages reported by the seven Croatian youths, only that portion of the reported occurring phenomena (*i.e.*, nature of apparitions, miraculous healings, solar miracles) which have a relevance to the content, either directly or by way of context, will be included here.

Further, it is important to understand that when the text contains phrases such as ''Mary stated'' or ''the message transmitted by Mary'', they are used to avoid the clumsiness of repetitive phrases such as ''the children said that Mary said that'' or ''the children reported that Mary transmitted''.

Finally, this study concerns only the contents of the message of Medjugorje and does not concern the numerous peripheral elements surrounding the Medjugorje event. Thereby, any matters regarding political, personal, or local ecclesiastical problematics are outside the scope of this study.

The focal point of this examination will be the following: that the message of Medjugorje is, in its foundational content, present in the Gospels of Sacred Scripture and the Apostolic Fathers; and, in its developmental content, present in the Documents of Vatican Council II and post-conciliar statements by the Magisterium of the Catholic Church; further, that the content of the message of Medjugorje is also consistent with the messages received at the ecclesiastically approved apparitions of the Blessed Virgin Mary at Lourdes, France in 1858 and at Fatima, Portugal in 1917.

The criterion of judgment, therefore, should address whether or not the reported messages by the Croatian youths attributed by them to Mary can in fact be found in the following sources:

1. Foundationally in the Gospels of Sacred Scripture, the inspired word of God, and in the writings of the Apostolic Fathers, the earliest non-canonical writings of the early Church;

2. Developmentally in the Documents of Vatican Council II and post-conciliar statements by the Magisterium, products of the living teaching office of the Catholic Church which is aided by the Holy Spirit in guarding and expounding faithfully the two-fold source of Divine Revelation, Sacred Scripture and Sacred Tradition;

3. Consistent and in no sense contradictory with the messages received during the Marian apparitions at Lourdes and at Fatima, which constitute ecclesiastically approved apparitions of the Blessed Virgin Mary.

Hence, the ultimate judgment to be made in this study is: can the contents of the messages reported by the Medjugorjian youths be found to be present in the aforementioned sources of Christian truth? It is the answer to this question that will comprise the subject of this investigation.

Before proceeding to the content of the message of Medjugorje, a brief introduction of the key figures involved in the present historical event will assist in understanding the identity and authority of those transmitting the messages.

The six youths reporting the apparitions of Mary nearly every day since June, 1981 and continuing at present (March, 1985), range in age from thirteen to twenty years of age. From youngest to oldest, the names of the youths are: Jakov Colo (male, born June 3, 1971), Ivanka Ivankovic (female, born April 21, 1966), Ivan Dragicevic (male, born May 25, 1965), Marija Pavlovic (female, born April 1, 1965), Mirjana Dragicevic (female, born March 18, 1965), and Vicka Ivankovic (female, born July 3, 1964). The six youths are referred to as the "visionaries", and report to see Mary in the form of a three-dimensional, external apparition.

Jelena Vasilj (female, born May 14, 1972) is frequently referred to as the "seventh visionary". Since December 15, 1982, Jelena has reported messages received from the Blessed Virgin Mary by means of inner locutions, seeing and hearing Mary, in Jelena's words, "with her heart". Jelena does not at present experience Mary in the external, three-dimensional manner as do the other six youths, nor does she share knowledge of the reported ''secrets'' given to the other youths by Mary.

The last relevant figure in this study is Father Tomislav Vlasic, O.F.M., a Franciscan priest who first visited the parish of St. James at Medjugorje five days after the reported beginnings of the apparitions, and was assigned there shortly after. Fr. Vlasic was the spiritual director of the visionaries during the first three years of the reported apparitions. Since that time, Fr. Vlasic has been reassigned to a neighboring parish in the diocese of Mostar.

Let us now proceed to the content of the messages reported by these seven Croatian youths from the small village town of Medjugorje, Yugoslavia—messages which they attribute to the Blessed Virgin Mary.

CHAPTER ONE

The Content of the Message of Medjugorje

Six youths from a small village in Yugoslavia known as Medjugorje (pronounced Med-ju-gor-ee-ay) have reported messages they attribute to the Blessed Virgin Mary during apparitions that began on June 24, 1981, and continue at the present time (March, 1985). These messages reported by the "visionaries" can be categorized into four basic divisions made by the author: 1. Personal Dialogue; 2. Secrets; 3. Information for Later Disclosure; and 4. Principals Messages.

The Personal Dialogue messages consist of discussions concerning the daily events of the visionaries, assistance in their individual spiritual lives, and also many personal questions or petitions brought to the visionaries by pilgrims requesting Mary's response. The intimate nature of these messages and their personal focus make them irrelevant to a general discussion of the content of the message of Medjugorje, but a few personal messages have been included because of their pertinence to the general body of content.

The division of the messages that constitutes the "Secrets" consists of ten secrets that Mary has promised to confide to the visionaries that, in substance, affect the entire world. At present (March, 1985), five children have received nine of the ten secrets, while Mirjana, the visionary who left Medjugorje to attend school in Sarajevo, has received all ten secrets. From the day she received the tenth secret (December 25, 1982) Mirjana no longer receives daily apparitions, but Mary has promised to appear to Mirjana every year on her birthday and during difficult times in her later life. Mirjana has transmitted the following message from Mary on the last day of her apparitions: "Now you have to turn to God through faith like everyone else. I will appear to you on your birthday, and when you encounter difficulties in life."[1] Since December 25, 1982, Mirjana has had only two apparitions of Mary, but occurring on her last two birthdays (March 18). Mirjana reports that Mary told her the dates of all the secrets, with the instructions to confide the secrets to the priest of her choosing three days before the event of each secret takes place.

All six visionaries state that the secrets have a global significance. Part of the first of the ten secrets has been disclosed by the youths. It consists of a sign promised by Mary that is to appear at the site of the first apparition (a nearby hill called ''Podbrdo''). In regards to this sign, there are a few specific messages of Mary. One message gives the motivation for the sign as an incentive for unbelievers: ''The sign will be given for the unbelievers. You faithful already have signs, and you yourselves must become the signs for the unbelievers.''[2] According to the visionaries, many healings and miracles will follow the sign, but for those who believe, the time that precedes the sign is not a time for waiting, but for a deeper conversion and faith: ''You faithful must not wait for the sign before you convert. Convert soon, for this time is a time of grace for you. You can never thank God enough for the grace God has given you. This time is for deepening your faith and your conversion. When the sign comes, it will be too late for many.''[3] Because of the obvious impossibility of a content analysis of the remaining nine secrets the category of the secrets also will not constitute a significant part of the subsequent discussion.

The third category of messages constitutes that information revealed to the visionaries for disclosure at a later time. This division includes confidential information that Mary is revealing to individual visionaries that is to be confided to Church authorities when such permission is given to them by Mary. For example, Vicka reports that she is being told aspects of Mary's own personal life, while Ivanka is being informed about future world events.[4] Due to the private nature of these messages, they likewise cannot comprise part of a content analysis of the messages.

It is therefore the fourth division of the messages, the Principal Messages, that will be the focus of this examination. The principal messages comprise those words spoken by Mary to the children that have a relevance not only to all Christians but to anyone who has, in the words of Mary, ''an open heart''. These messages are conveyed through the six visionaries, either collectively or as individuals, and are the product of Mary's appearances and communication with them. The second source of principal messages are those transmitted through Jelena Vasilj, the ''seventh visionary''. As previously explained, Jelena has reported messages from Mary that reach her through the gift of inner locutions, seeing and hearing Mary, as she describes, ''with her heart.'' The nature of the messages transmitted through Jelena oftentimes take the form of implementing and interiorizing the general messages received by the other six youths. Along with Jelena, there is another girl, Marijana Vasilj (no relation), who reports the same type of charism as Jelena, but the nature of her dialogue with Mary at present seems to be primarily that of a personal spiritual direction.

The messages reported by the visionaries and attributed to the Blessed Virgin Mary actually began on June 25, 1981, the second day of the apparitions. The first day of the apparitions, when the youths reported seeing Mary at two different times, they were not accompanied by any verbal message. From the second day of the apparitions to the present, Mary has transmitted to the children numerous verbal messages, but they have not been recorded in any comprehensive or methodical manner since the confiscation of the rectory's records by the local police authorities towards the beginning of the apparitions. Hence, the messages will appear with as much chronological data that is available. All messages that follow have been approved as accurate by the priests of the parish of St. James at Medjugorje.

Messages of the First Seven Days, June 24 to June 30, 1981

June 25, 1981: The first words spoken by Mary to the youths occurred on the second day of the apparitions, and they pertained to a specific question concerning the state of Ivanka's mother who had died two months earlier. Mary responded that her mother is well, is with her, and that Ivanka should not worry.[5] Ivanka then asked whether her mother had any message for her children, to which Mary spoke the words: "Obey your grandmother and be good to her, for she is old and cannot work."[6] Mary ended the apparition with the words: "Go in God's peace."[7]

June 26, 1981: On the third day of the apparitions, Vicka began the dialogue by sprinkling holy water upon the apparition and saying, "If you are really Our Lady, then stay with us. If not, leave us."[8] Mary's response was a smile.[9] The children then asked Mary who she was, and why she had come to their village. Mary responded: "I am the Blessed Virgin Mary." She continued, "I am here because there are many good believers here. I want to be with you, and to convert and reconcile all people."[10] The visionaries also reported an apparition later in the day where Mary repeated the parting words: "Go in God's peace."[11]

As one of the visionaries, Marija, was walking home from that evening apparition, she reported a further apparition of Mary positioned in front of a cross without a corpus, and with tears in her eyes. Mary spoke the words: "Peace, peace, peace . . . nothing but peace. Men must be reconciled with God and with one another. For this to happen, it is necessary to believe, to pray, to fast, and to go to Confession. Go in God's peace."[12]

June 27, 1981: The fourth day of the apparitions brought the following questions from the children and these answers from Mary:

Father Jozo Zovko, O.F.M., at that time the pastor of St. James parish at Medjugorje, instructed the children to ask Mary whether she had any specific messages for priests. Mary responded: "Let the priests firmly believe."[13]

Vicka asked Mary to prove to the other people present at the site of the apparition that she was truly present. Mary stated: "Let those who do not see believe as if they see."[14]

Mirjana was troubled over the accusations from other local people that the youths were drug addicts or epileptics. When she expressed this concern to Mary, the response was: "There has always been injustice in the world, and there will always be. Disregard it."[15]

Ivanka asked Mary her name. Again Mary answered: "I am the Blessed Virgin Mary."[16] Upon leaving, Mary said: "Go in God's peace."[17] During a later vision during that same day, Mary said to the youths: "You are my angels, my dear angels. . . . Go in God's peace."[18]

June 28, 1981: On day five of the apparitions, the visionaries and Mary had another dialogue of considerable length:

Visionaries:	Dear Madonna! What do you wish from us?
Mary:	Faith and respect for me.
Visionaries:	Dear Madonna! Why don't you appear in the church so that everybody sees you?
Mary:	Blessed are they who have not seen and have believed.
Visionaries:	Dear Madonna! Will you come again?
	Mary nodded, but did not reply.
Visionaries:	Dear Madonna! Do you prefer us to pray to you or to sing to you?
Mary:	Do both, sing and pray.
Visionaries:	Dear Madonna! What do you wish from these people who have gathered here?
Mary:	Let them believe as if they had seen.

At this point in the dialogue, Mary left. The children thought that Mary would return, since she had not said her usual parting words, "Go in God's peace". As the children began praying, Mary appeared a second time. The children began to sing a traditional Marian song to her, at which point the dialogue resumed:

Mary:	My angels, my dear angels.
Visionaries:	Dear Madonna! What do you wish from these people here?
Mary:	Let these people who do not see me believe in the same way as the six of you who see me.
Visionaries:	Dear Madonna! Shall you leave us some sign here on the earth so that we may convince these people that we are not liars, that we do not lie, that we are not merely playing around with you?

Mary: Go in God's peace.[19]

The children also asked Mary on this day how she would like them to pray. Mary responded: "Continue to recite seven times the Our Father, Hail Mary, Glory Be, and the Creed."[20]

June 29, 1981 On the sixth day, the youths had the following conversation with Mary that includes a request for the healing of a three-year-old child, Danijel Setka, who was unable to speak due to an infant paralysis:

Visionaries:	Dear Madonna! Are you glad that the people are here? *Mary smiles in confirmation.*
Visionaries:	Dear Madonna! How many days are you going to stay with us?
Mary:	As long as you wish.
Visionaries:	Dear Madonna! Are you going to leaves us any sign?
Mary:	I am going to come again tomorrow.
Visionaries:	Dear Madonna! What do you wish from these people?
Mary:	There is only one God and one faith. Believe firmly.
Visionaries:	Are we going to be able to endure this? Many are persecuting us because we see. . . .
Mary:	You will, my angels.
Visionaries:	Dear Madonna! What wish do you have for us here?
Mary:	That you have firm faith and confidence.
Visionaries:	Dear Madonna! Can this lady [Dr. Darinka Glamuzina sent from Citluk to investigate] touch you?
Mary:	There have always been unfaithful Judases. Let her come.
Visionaries:	(to the crowd) She is touching her. . . . She left! She left! (The children resume singing with the crowd and Mary returns.) Light! Light! Here she is! Here she is!
Visionaries:	Dear Madonna. Will this little boy Danijel ever be able to speak? Do a miracle so that all will believe us. Dear Madonna. Do a miracle. . . . Dear Madonna. Say something.
Visionaries:	Dear Madonna. Say something, we ask you. Say something dear Madonna.
Mary:	Let them (Danijel's parents) firmly believe that he will be healed. Go in God's peace.[21]*

June 30, 1981: The messages conveyed to the children by Mary on the seventh day of the apparitions are taken from an interview between the youths and Father Jozo Zovko, O.F.M., the parish pastor at the time. The interview immediately followed the apparition:

* The parents of Danijel Setka reported the cure of their son at the beginning of November, 1981.

Fr. Jozo:	Mirjana, what did you talk about with the Madonna?
Mirjana:	I asked her if she minds that we went from the hill and came to the other place [in the church]. She said that she does not mind.
Ivanka:	We asked if she is going to leave us some sign. She simply and slowly left and again the light was on the hill where the people were.
Mirjana:	And she said: "Go in God's peace."
Jakov:	She also said: "My angels"; when we asked if she is going to mind appearing to us in the church, she said: "I will not, my angels."[22]

Messages from July, 1981
to December, 1983

From June 30, 1981 to July 3, 1981, the apparitions took place in the parish rectory. After July 3, the exact sites and dates of the apparitions are not recorded, although the apparitions continued daily. The following messages are those that possess some chronological data, and they will be followed by messages within this same approximate period (July, 1981 to December, 1983) that have been approved as accurate, but without any specific date of transmittance.

August 6, 1981: The attestations of numerous witnesses, both pilgrims and townspeople, state that the word "MIR" (Croatian for "PEACE") was written in the sky above the hill. This sign has been reported on several other occasions.[23]

August 7, 1981: The youths reported that Mary had asked them to go to the top of the mountain of the cross (a neighboring mountain where in 1933 the townspeople had built a large, concrete cross commemorating the 1900th anniversary of the crucifixion of Christ) at approximately two o'clock in the morning to pray that the people would do penance for sinners. She then promised to give a special sign so that the world would believe.[24]

August, 1981: The youths asked Mary what was the "best fast". Mary answered: "A fast of bread and water."[25]

End of August, 1981: Mary conveyed these words concerning her title: "I am the Queen of Peace."[26]

September 4, 1981: Concerning the sign for unbelievers, Mary specified that this sign would be given after the termination of the apparitions.[27]

October, 1981: Ivica Vego, a priest from Mostar, asked the visionaries to ask Mary the following three questions. Question 1. What will happen in and to Poland? Mary replied: "There will soon be great conflicts there, but in the end the righteous will triumph."[28]

Question 2. Will the "case of Hercegovina" be resolved satisfactorily (a reference to the controversy between the Franciscan Order and the episcopal authority in Hercegovina)? Mary responded: "The problem will be resolved satisfactorily. There is need of prayer and penance."[29]

Question 3 pertained to the world conflict between the East and West, to which Mary answered: "Russia is the people where God will be most glorified. The West has advanced in civilization, but without God, as though it were its own creator."[30] Mary's message concerning the West continued, but Marija, the visionary who voiced the questions and received the answers, was unable to disclose the rest, as if it would have disclosed an aspect of the secrets.

October 22, 1981: Many people reported seeing the large concrete cross on the top of the mountain turn to a pillar of light with the figure of a woman, as a statue, at the foot of the cross. This continued for approximately thirty minutes, and was proceeded by the following message from Mary: "All these signs are to reinforce your faith until I send the permanent, visible sign."[31]

December 7, 1981: In regard to the implementation of her call for conversion, Mary said: "Many people are on the way to conversion, but not all."[32]

December 8, 1981 (Feast of the Immaculate Conception): The visionaries saw Mary on her knees, praying these words: "My beloved Son. Please forgive these numerous sins with which humanity is offending You." After praying with the children, Mary told them that she is praying daily at the foot of the cross, asking her Son to forgive humanity of its sins.[33]

January, 1982: At the beginning of the month, Mary was again seen at the foot of the cross in a position of prayer by several pilgrims and priests. Fr. Tomislav Vlasic, spiritual director of the visionaries, requested the youths to inquire of Mary whether it was in fact she at the foot of the cross located upon the mountain. The message conveyed was: "It is understandable that I am praying at the foot of the cross. The cross is a sign of salvation. My Son suffered on the cross; He redeemed the world on the cross. Salvation comes from the cross."[34]

July 21, 1982: As to the power of prayer and fasting, the following words were transmitted: "Christians have forgotten that they can prevent war and even natural calamaties by prayer and fasting."[35]

August 6, 1982: The visionaries reported Mary's message on this day to be a recommendation for monthly Confession, which was immediately implemented by the parish.[36]

August, 1982: Ivan, one of the visionaries, was on the hillside with

friends, when Mary appeared to him and spoke the following words:
"Now I will give you a sign to strengthen your faith." Ivan reported two
bright beams of light coming down, one that rested upon the church, the
other upon the cross on the mountain. The same phenomenon was
reported by Ivan's friends.[37]

Spring, 1983: Again, on the subject of conversion and a deepening of
faith, Mary exhorted with these words: "Hasten your conversion. Do not
wait for the sign that has been announced for the unbelievers, it will
already be too late for them to have a conversion. You who believe, be
converted, and deepen your faith."[38]

April 20, 1983: A further call for world conversion: "The only word I
wish to speak of is the conversion of the whole world. I wish to speak it to
you so that you can speak it to the whole world. I ask nothing but
conversion. . . . It is my desire . . . be converted . . . leave everything;
that comes from conversion. Good-bye now, and may peace be with
you."[39]

Messages from July, 1981 to December, 1983
Without Specific Chronological Data

The following messages comprise those for which no specific chronological data is available apart from that general time-period between July,
1981 and December, 1983.[40]

The visionaries report Mary's opening greeting as most always being,
"Praised be Jesus." The visionaries respond by the phrase, "May Jesus
and Mary always be praised."

In response to a question concerning the possible need of a parish
prayer group, Mary stated: "Yes, there is a need for a prayer group not
only in this parish, but in all parishes. Spiritual renewal is needed for the
entire Church."[41]

Responding to requests for healing from pilgrims, the visionaries
transmitted: "I myself cannot heal you. Only God Himself can heal you.
Pray, I will pray with you. Firmly believe, fast, and do penance. I will
help you as much as it is in my power. God is helping everybody; I am not
God. I need your prayers and sacrifices to help me."[42]

The children reported a complaint from Mary regarding the number of
believers who never pray. She asked the children to call the people to
prayer, stating: "Faith cannot be alive without prayer."[43]

Mary stated that the best prayer was the Creed. When asked about the
Mass, Mary responded: "The Mass is the greatest prayer from God, and
you will never understand the greatness of it. Therefore, you must be
perfect and humble at Mass, and you must be prepared for it."[44]

The visionaries asked whether people should be praying to Jesus or to her. The answer: "Please pray to Jesus. I am His Mother and I intercede for you to Him. But all prayers go to Jesus. I will help, I will pray, but everything does not depend on me, but also on your strength—the strength of those who pray."[45]*

The children reported that Mary has shown them Heaven, Hell, and Purgatory (though not all the children saw Purgatory and Hell, at their own request). While showing them Purgatory, Mary stated: "Those people are waiting for your prayers and sacrifices." While some of the children were shown Hell, Mary's words were: "This is the punishment for those who do not love God; and many who are alive today will go to Hell."[46]

Responding to special requests from pilgrims, Mary oftentimes has given the same answer: there is no special prayer for special needs. Prayer, penance, and fasting are the conditions for healing ailments of both body and soul. Nevertheless, people may mention a particular petition when praying either for themselves or for others.[47]

Mary has requested that everyone pray daily the seven Our Fathers, seven Hail Mary's, seven Glory Be's and the Creed. These prayers are to be said, not in the place of but in addition to the other prayers promulgated by the Church. She has frequently encouraged praying the Rosary, and she has emphasized the fact that every prayer is pleasing to God. Further, she insists that the times when Mary and the children pray in unison do not conflict with the parish-appointed times for Mass.[48]

Mary has complained that the practice of fasting in the Church has almost disappeared. She wants believers to fast on Fridays on bread and water only.** Fasting and prayer are constantly emphasized as the most powerful means to conversion. She has stated that the giving of alms by the healthy does not constitute a legitimate substitution for fasting.[49]

Regarding the seriously ill, or a person in serious sin, Mary has transmitted to the visionaries the recommendation of people uniting in prayer for these intentions. Those who are too ill to fast for themselves can choose some other form of sacrifice, together with the reception of the sacraments of Confession and Holy Communion.[50]

In reference to the promised sign for unbelievers and the specific belief of the visionaries, Mary stated: "You do not need a sign, you must be a sign."[51]

---

* The mention of Mary that "all prayers go to Jesus" seems to point more to the ultimate recipient of prayer, namely, Christ, by way of Mary's role as intercessor, than to any prohibition of prayer said directly to Mary. The call to pray the Rosary and to consecrate oneself to the Immaculate Heart of Mary would support this conclusion.

** Mary's Thursday message of August 14, 1984 that will appear later in this chapter adds Wednesdays to the Friday fasts of bread and water.

The visionaries have reported that many miracles will accompany the arrival of the sign. And in reference to a determinate perseverance in living out the message, Mary stated: "I know many will not believe you and many enthused for the faith will grow cold. You should stay steadfast and urge the people to steadfast prayer, penance, and conversion. In the end, you will be the happiest."[52]

Regarding the diversity of religions, the visionaries reported this message: "In God's eyes there are no divisions and there are no religions. You in the world have made the divisions. The one mediator is Jesus Christ. Which religion you belong to cannot be a matter of indifference. The presence of the Holy Spirit is not the same in every Church."[53]

Mary has described the Sacrament of Reconciliation as: ". . . a medicine for the Church in the West. . . . Whole regions of the Church would be healed if believers would go to Confession once a month."[54]

On several occasions, the children have reported Mary appearing with Christ, either as a child or in His Passion, and accompanied with the following words: "Do whatever He tells you."[55]

Interview with Mirjana Dragicevic
January 10, 1983

The following interview with Mirjana, one of the six visionaries (age 19 at the time of the interview) was held by Fr. Tomislav Vlasic, O.F.M., spiritual director of the visionaries, on January 10, 1983. These statements possess a particular relevance to the general body of the message content, arising from the fact that Mirjana is the only visionary who reports to have received all ten secrets (at which time she ceased receiving the apparitions). Further Mirjana alone has reported a personal encounter with Satan, which adds further information and content to the principal messages. This interview has been edited by the author from a content-oriented perspective:[56]

Fr. Vlasic: Mirjana, we have not seen each other for some time, and I would like you to tell me about the apparitions of the Blessed Virgin Mary, and especially the events connected with you.

Mirjana: I have seen the Blessed Virgin Mary for eighteen months now, and I feel I know her well. I feel she loves me with her motherly love, and so I have been able to ask her about everything I would like to know. I've asked her to explain some things about Heaven, Purgatory, and Hell that were not clear to me. For example, I asked her how God can be so unmerciful as to throw people into Hell, to suffer forever. I thought: if a person commits a crime and goes to jail, he stays there for a while and then is forgiven—but to Hell, forever? She told me that souls who go to Hell have ceased thinking favorably of God—have cursed Him, and more and more. So they've already become part of Hell, and chosen not to be delivered from it. Then she told me that there are levels in Purgatory: levels closer to Hell and higher and higher toward Heaven. Most people, she said, think many souls are released from Purgatory into Heaven on All Saints' Day, but most souls are taken into Heaven on Christmas Day.

Fr. Vlasic: Did you ask why God allows Hell?

Mirjana: No I did not. But afterwards I had a discussion with my aunt, who told me how merciful God is. So I said I would ask the Madonna how God could. . . .

Fr. Vlasic: According to what you've said, then, it's as simple as this: people who oppose God on earth just continue their existence after death, and oppose God in Hell?

Mirjana: Really, I thought if a person goes to Hell. . . . Don't people pray for their salvation? Could God be so unmerciful as not to hear their prayers? Then the Madonna explained it to me. People in Hell do not pray at all; instead, they blame God for everything. In effect, they become one with that Hell and they get used to it. They rage against God, and they suffer, but they always refuse to pray to God.

Fr. Vlasic: To ask Him for salvation?

Mirjana: In Hell, they hate Him even more.

Fr. Vlasic: As for Purgatory, you say that souls who pray frequently are sometimes allowed to communicate, at least by messages, with people on earth, and that they receive the benefits of prayers said on earth?

Mirjana: Yes. Prayers that are said on earth for souls who have not prayed for their salvation are applied to souls in Purgatory who pray for their salvation.

Fr. Vlasic: Did the Madonna tell you whether many people go to Hell today?

Mirjana: I asked her about that recently, and she said that, today, most people go to Purgatory, the next greatest number go to Hell, and only a few go directly to Heaven.

Fr. Vlasic:	Only a few go to Heaven?
Mirjana:	Yes. Only a few—the least number—go to Heaven.
Fr. Vlasic:	Purgatory?
Mirjana:	I didn't see Purgatory either. Just Heaven. But the Madonna described Purgatory as I told you—with levels.
Fr. Vlasic:	Well, besides Heaven, Hell, and Purgatory, is there anything else new recently?
Mirjana:	The Madonna told me that I should tell the people that many in our time judge their faith by their priests. If a priest is not holy, they conclude that there is no God. She said: "You do not go to church to judge the priest, to examine his personal life. You go to church to pray and to hear the Word of God from the priest." This must be explained to the people, because many turn away from the faith because of priests.
	Today, as it was a long time ago, the Virgin told me God and the devil conversed, and the devil said that people believe in God only when life is good for them. When things turn bad, they cease to believe in God. Then people blame God, or act as if does not exist.
	God, therefore, allowed the devil one century in which to exercise an extended power over the world, and the devil chose the twentieth century. Today, as we see all around us, everyone is dissatisfied; they cannot live with each other. Examples are the number of divorces and abortions. All this, the Madonna said, is the work of the devil.
Fr. Vlasic:	You have said that the devil has entered into some marriages. Is his rule limited to those marriages?
Mirjana:	No. This is just the beginning.
Fr. Vlasic:	This behavior of people—they're under the influence of the devil. But the devil does not have to be in them?
Mirjana:	No, no. The devil is not in them, but they're under the influence of the devil, although he enters into some of them. To prevent this, at least to some extent, the Madonna said we need communal prayer, family prayer. She stressed the need for family prayer, most of all. Also, every family should have at least one sacred object in the house, and houses should be blessed regularly. She also emphasized the failings of religious people, especially in small villages—for example, here in Medjugorje, where there is a separation from

Serbians and Moslems. This separation is not good. The Madonna always stresses that there is but one God, and that people have enforced unnatural separation. One cannot truly believe, be a true Christian, if he does not respect other religions as well. You do not really believe in God if you make fun of other religions.

Fr. Vlasic: What, then, is the role of Jesus Christ, if the Moslem religion is a good religion?

Mirjana: We did not discuss that. She merely explained, and deplored, the lack of religious unity, "especially in the villages". She said that everybody's religion should be respected, and of course one's own.

Fr. Vlasic: Tell me where the devil is especially active today. Did she tell you anything about this? Through whom or what does he manifest himself the most?

Mirjana: Most of all through people of weak character, who are divided within themselves. Such people are everywhere, and they are the easiest for the devil to enter. But he also enters the lives of strong believers—sisters, for example. He would rather "convert" real believers than non-believers. How can I explain this? You saw what happened to me. He tries to bring as many believers as possible to himself.

Fr. Vlasic: What do you mean, "What happened to me"? Is that what you talked about before?

Mirjana: Yes.

Fr. Vlasic: You have never discussed what happened into my tape recorder. Please try to describe it now, so I can record it.

Mirjana: It was approximately six months ago, though I don't know exactly and cannot say for sure. As usual, I had locked myself into my room, alone, and waited for the Madonna. I knelt down, and had not yet made the sign of the cross, when suddenly a bright light flashed and the devil appeared. It was as if something told me it was the devil. I looked at him and was very surprised, for I was expecting the Madonna to appear. He was horrible—he was black, all over and he had. . . . He was terrifying, dreadful, and I did not know what he wanted. I realized I was growing weak, and then I fainted. When I revived, he was still standing there, laughing. It seemed that he game me a strange kind of strength, so that I could almost accept him. He told me that I would be very beautiful, and very happy, and so on. However, I would have no need of the Madonna, he said, and no need for faith. "She has brought you nothing but suffering and difficulties," he said; but he would give me everything beautiful—whatever I want. Then something in me—I don't know what, if it was something conscious or something in my soul—told me: *No! No! No!* Then I began to shake and feel just awful. Then he disappeared, and the Madonna appeared, and when she appeared my strength returned—as if she restored it to me. I felt normal again. Then the Madonna told me: "That was a trial, but it will not happen to you again."

Fr. Vlasic: Did the Madonna say anything else?

Mirjana: Nothing else. She told me it would not happen again and that she would talk to me about it later.

Fr. Vlasic: You said that the twentieth century has been given over to the devil?

Mirjana: Yes.

Fr. Vlasic: You mean the century until the year 2000, or generally speaking?

Mirjana: Generally, part of which is in the twentieth century, until the first secret is unfolded. The devil will rule til then. She told me several secrets and explained them to me; and I have written them down in code letters, with dates, so I won't forget them. If, say, tomorrow a secret is to be revealed, I have a right, two or three days before, to pick whatever priest I want and tell him about it. For example: "The day after tomorrow, such-and-such will happen." The priest, then, is free to do as he thinks best with that information. He can write it out before it happens, then read it to others after it happens. He can also tell it to the people: "Tomorrow, such-and-such will happen." It's up to him to decide what to do with the information."

Fr. Vlasic: Were these secrets ever revealed before, to anybody in previous generations?

Mirjana I can't answer that. Anyway, you know all the secrets that have been told before. You do not know all the secrets I have been told. You know some of them, but not all.[57]

Fr. Vlasic: So then, I don't know all of them; but since you've been told not to talk about them, I won't ask you to.

That's all right—as it should be. But I'll ask you if you know when the secrets will be revealed?

Mirjana: I know. I know every date of every secret.

Fr. Vlasic: But you can't say anything about this?

Mirjana: I can't.

Fr. Vlasic: Can we suppose, then, that one of you might say that three secrets would be revealed before the great sign appears; then, the rest of the secrets will be revealed, one by one? Is there anything to that?

Mirjana: Nothing like that, but something like this. First, some secrets will be revealed—just a few. Then, then the people will be convinced that the Madonna was here. Then they will understand the sign. When Jakov said that the mayor will be the first one to run to the hill, he meant generally, people of the highest social class. They will understand the sign as a place or occasion to convert. They will run to the hill and pray, and they will be forgiven. When I asked the Madonna about unbelievers, she said: "They should be prayed for, and they should pray." But when I asked again, recently, she said: "Let them convert while there is time." She did not say they should be prayed for.

Fr. Vlasic: You can say nothing specifically until the moment the Madonna says you can?

Mirjana: Yes.

Fr. Vlasic: Can we say that some of the secrets belong only to you, personally?

Mirjana: No. None of the secrets is personally for me.

Fr. Vlasic: Not you, then, but Ivan has received personal secrets.

Mirjana: My secrets are for all mankind generally, for the world. Medjugorje, some other areas, and about the sign.

Fr. Vlasic: The sign will pertain to this parish?

Mirjana: Yes, to Medjugorje. But there is something else.

Fr. Vlasic: Something else?

Mirjana: Nothing for me personally.

Fr. Vlasic: You have been given the last of the secrets?

Mirjana: Yes, the tenth.

Fr. Vlasic: Can you tell me what it relates to?

Mirjana: I cannot; but I can tell you that the eighth secret is worse than the other seven. I prayed for a long time that it might be less severe. Every day, when the Madonna came, I pestered her, asking that it be mitigated. Then she said that everyone should pray that it might be lessened. So, in Sarajevo, I got many people to join me in this prayer. Later, the Madonna told me that she'd been able to have the secret lessened. But then she told me the ninth secret and it was even worse. The tenth secret is totally bad and cannot be lessened whatsoever. I cannot say anything about it, because even a word would disclose the secret before it's time to do so.

Fr. Vlasic: I won't press you. Anyway, though, the tenth secret has to do with what will definitely happen?

Mirjana: Yes, prepare! The Madonna said people should prepare themselves spiritually, be ready, and not panic; be reconciled in their souls. They should be ready for the worst, to die tomorrow. They should accept God now so that they will not be afraid. They should accept God and everything else. No one accepts death easily, but they can be at peace in their souls if they are believers. If they are committed to God, he will accept them.

Fr. Vlasic: This means total conversion and surrender to God?

Mirjana: Yes.

Fr. Vlasic: After these ten secrets, after these eighteen months of apparitions, what do you tell the people they should do? What do you say to priests, to the Pope and bishops, without revealing the secrets? What does the Madonna want us to do?

Mirjana: First, I would like to tell you how it was for me at the end, and the. . .

Fr. Vlasic: All right.

Mirjana: Two days before Christmas, the Madonna told me Christmas Day would be the last time she would appear to me (I didn't quite believe this). On Christmas Day, she stayed with me for forty-five minutes, and we talked about many things. We summarized everything that had been said between us. On behalf of many people, I asked what they should do. Then she gave me a very precious gift: she said she would appear to me on my birthday every year for the rest of my life. Also, independently of the sign—and everything else—she said that she will appear to me when something very difficult happens—not some everyday difficulty, but something quite grievous. Then she will come to help me. But now, I have to live without her physical presence, without her daily, personal visits. I say to all people: Convert!—the same as she said; ''Convert while there is time!'' Do not abandon God and your faith. Abandon everything else, but not that! I ask priests to help their people, because priests can cause them to reject their faith. After a man has been ordained, he must really be a priest, bringing people to the Church. The most important point is that the people convert and pray.

Fr. Vlasic: What is the greatest danger to mankind? What does it come from?

Mirjana: From godlessness. Nobody believes—hardly anybody. For example, the Madonna told me that the faith in Germany, Switzerland, and Austria is very weak. The people in these countries model themselves on their priests, and if the priests are not good examples, the people fall away and believe there is no God. When I was in A. . . , I heard of a priest to whom a rich man had left money to build a home for old people, but instead the priest built a hotel. Now all the people in that city have turned their backs on the faith, because how could a priest not fulfill the last wish of a dying man and, instead, built a hotel and make money for himself? Nevertheless, people must understand that they shouldn't scrutinize a priest's private life, but listen to what he says through God—God's word.

Fr. Vlasic: Why did the Madonna introduce herself as the Queen of Peace?

Mirjana: You know very well that the situation in the world is horrible. There are wars in every part of the world. The situation is very tense. Peace is needed—a just and simple peace. First, peace in the soul; then. . .

Fr. Vlasic: So the message of the Madonna is a message of peace?

Mirjana: Yes. Primarily peace of the soul. If a person has it in his soul, he is surrounded by it.

Fr. Vlasic: Peace comes as a result of faith in God and surrender to him.

Mirjana: Yes, as a consequence of prayer, penance, and fasting.

Fr. Vlasic: The Madonna tells us that peace can be achieved that way; but evil things will happen nevertheless. Why?

Mirjana: They have to happen. The world has become very evil.

It cares about faith very little. A little while ago, I told you what she said when I decided to wear a cross around my neck. How many city people will say with approval: "What a sensible girl", and how many will say instead: "How stupid she is."

Fr. Vlasic: I do not remember your saying that to me.

Mirjana: The Madonna was telling me at length how faith has declined. For example, now I live in the provincial capital, Sarajevo, and if I put a simple cross pendant around my neck and walked on the streets, how many people would say, or think to themselves, "What a sensible girl!", and what proportion would say or think, "What a stupid or old-fashioned girl"? Nowadays, people curse God, Jesus Christ, his Mother, his Father, day in and day out, habitually. Besides, people have fallen into very evil ways, so that they live in evil routinely. It's no wonder that God is at the end of his patience.

Fr. Vlasic: Why do you think the Blessed Mary always exhorts the world, over and over again, to prayer and penance?

Mirjana: When we pray, we pray to God (that's what you said in your sermon last night). In return, we receive peace of soul, tranquility. We have opened our hearts to God, so that God can enter, and when we have God in our heart and soul, we cannot cause evil to anybody. We will not curse—do anything evil. We will do good.

Fr. Vlasic: But the Madonna also says that we should pray for others.

Mirjana: We have to pray for anyone we see who is. . . . For example, I always pray for non-believers, because they do not know what is missing in their lives. They have no idea of how much they may have to suffer later. I pray that God will convert them, that He will give them a sign, that He will open their souls so that they can accept the faith.

Fr. Vlasic: I understand that, with prayer, we open ourselves to God, but the Madonna always seems to stress the need for prayer for others—prayer and fasting. Do you think that prayer and fasting bring a proper balance into the world? Do you feel that prayer and fasting can even partially atone for all the sins of the world?

Mirjana: Yes, I do; it's possible. Much can be done through prayer and fasting. The Madonna has said that prayer can stop wars and prevent catastrophes. Prayer and fasting! Of course prayer can help a struggling human who does not accept God and religion. Moreover, we are obliged to pray that such a person's heart will be opened. Again, I talk to many non-believers in Sarajevo and try to explain things to them so that they will gain at least a little understanding. Sometimes, it is not their fault; they received no religious training when they were young. Or later, when they abandoned their faith, no one tried to help them. I pray that God will open such hearts.

Fr. Vlasic: Have you received any special messages for priests and bishops?

Mirjana: No, but a long time ago she said that they should accept us, help us as much as they can, and pray more and do penance.

Fr. Vlasic: Priests and bishops too?

Mirjana: Yes.

Fr. Vlasic: So you were given no special message for any priest?

Mirjana: No. Not exactly.

Fr. Vlasic: For the Pope?

Mirjana: No. I never asked about the Pope.

Mirjana: Maybe I can tell you about when she stopped appearing to me.

Fr. Vlasic: Yes?

Mirjana: I asked her why, why I had to be the first. She said that she stayed with us for a long time, longer than is necessary, but that this is the last apparition on earth. . . .

Fr. Vlasic: What do you mean, "the last apparition on earth"?

Mirjana: It is the last time that Jesus or Mary will appear on earth.

Fr. Vlasic What do you mean, "appear"?

Mirjana: The last time they will appear as they have, so that you can speak with them.

Fr. Vlasic: You mean that this is the last apparition in this era, in this period of the Church, or that they will never again come to earth?

Mirjana: I don't know. She said she will not appear on earth. I do not know if she means this era. I do not know how to ask such a question properly.

Fr. Vlasic: Did you ever ask about other apparitions in the world— the Madonna's apparitions in our time at other places?

Mirjana: She mentioned a man in Germany who caused panic

among the people—on buses, trains and the like—telling them: "Convert! While there is still time!" There are many false prophets in our time, she said, throughout the world, who lie, claiming to see the Madonna or Jesus. This is a great sin, and we should pray for such people. In fact, she and I prayed for fourteen days, exclusively, for false prophets. They do not understand how grave a sin it is to lie about having visions.

Fr. Vlasic: If you had decided to enter a convent and live the life of a religious, would she continue to appear. What do you think?

Mirjana: I think she would, but I'm not sure. But maybe she wouldn't! She has already stayed on earth too long, she said, and hadn't intended to stay even this length of time. So I can't say what she would do if I went into a convent instead of a continuing school. Anyway, she promised me this marvelous gift on my birthdays.

Fr. Vlasic: She did not mention further developments or apparitions, either individually or to all of you as a group?

Mirjana: I think that when each individual learns the tenth secret, she will cease appearing to that person.

Fr. Vlasic: Can you, nevertheless [in spite of the termination of the apparitions for Mirjana]—in your prayers, in your inner self—feel some sense of her presence?

Mirjana: Yes, I can! I felt her last night, when we prayed the seven Our Fathers. The feeling was beautiful, as if I were praying with her. It was as if I heard her voice in my heart, echoing in me and praying together with me. I was aware of nothing around me. I simply immersed myself in praying, as she does. I heard our two voices echoing.

Fr. Vlasic: Did you really hear her voice, or did it just seem that you heard her?

Mirjana: I can't say for sure. When I prayed, I heard her voice as I told you. Even though I was completely immersed in prayer, I heard her, her resonant voice. It was exactly as if she was praying with me. It was praying the Our Father from the beginning, not just the second half. I prayed the other prayers, too, and it was exactly as if she was with me.

Fr. Vlasic: Did you hear her voice in your ears, or—somehow—in your heart?

Mirjana: In my soul.

Fr. Vlasic: The Madonna said that if we pray for a particular need. . .

Mirjana: We should emphasize exactly that: "Dear God, I'm praying to be healed of my illness." Pray like that. But pray from your heart, from the bottom of your soul, with feeling. It does not have to be a "regular" prayer, but a conversation with God. "God, you see my suffering. You know how I am. I'm not complaining, my cross is not too difficult to bear; but I would like to be on my feet again so I can move around in the world." Like that: conversation, then prayer.

Fr. Vlasic: Did the Madonna ever recommend special devotions?

Mirjana: She always recommended faith, prayer, and penance. She never mentioned anything special for anybody, whether they were sick or healthy. But, as I told you, she said we should direct our prayers: "I am praying for such-and-such." And we should pray with concentration, not race through the words of Our Father. The main thing is not to say the words of a prayer, but to feel them.

Fr. Vlasic: And fasting?

Mirjana: She said that sick people do not have to fast. If they do not fast, it is not a sin for them. They can do another good deed instead. For those who are able to fast, it is not enough that they do a good deed instead.

Fr. Vlasic: Does she say fasting must be on bread and water only, or are other kinds of fasting acceptable?

Mirjana: We did not discuss fasting except on bread and water. But probably she meant we should fast only on bread and water.

Fr. Vlasic: Everybody?

Mirjana: Yes—everybody who wants to receive something from God or have God's help.

Fr. Vlasic: Are there any other points you want to mention.

Mirjana: Not that I can remember.

Account of the Message of Medjugorje
Sent to Pope John Paul II by Fr. Tomislav Vlasic
and the Visionaries, November 30, 1983

In November of 1983, Marija Pavlovic, one of the visionaries, reported the request of Mary to inform the Pope and the local bishop as to the urgency and importance of her messages to the visionaries. Accordingly, Fr. Vlasic, in conjunction with the visionaries, sent the following report to Pope John Paul II. This later synthesis of the content of the messages accentuates an urgency not present in any of the earlier formulations of the context (with the possible exception of Mirjana's interview). The report appears here in its entirety:[58]

Report Sent to Rome
by the Parish of Medjugorje

After the apparition of the Blessed Virgin on November 30, 1983, Marija Pavlovic came to me and said, "The Madonna says that the Supreme Pontiff and the Bishops must be advised immediately of the urgency and great importance of the message of Medjugorje."

This letter seeks to fulfill that duty.

1. Five young people (Vicka Ivankovic, Marija Pavlovic, Ivanka Ivankovic, Ivan Dragicevic, and Jakov Colo) see an apparition of the Blessed Virgin every day. The experience in which they see her is a fact that can be checked by direct observation. It has been filmed. During the apparitions, the youngsters do not react to light, they do not hear sounds, they do not react if someone touches them, they feel that they are beyond time and space.

"We see the Blessed Virgin just as we see anyone else. We pray with her, we speak to her, and we can touch her."

"The Blessed Virgin says that world peace is at a critical stage. She repeatedly calls for reconciliation and conversion."

"She has promised to leave a visible sign for all humanity at the site of the apparitions of Medjugorje."

"The period preceding this visible sign is a time of grace for conversion and deepening the faith."

"The Blessed Virgin has promised to disclose ten secrets to us. So far, Vicka Ivankovic has received eight. Marija Pavlovic received the ninth one on December 8, 1983. Jakov Colo, Ivan Dragicevic and Ivanka Ivankovic have each received nine. Only Mirjana Dragicevic has received all ten."

"These apparitions are the last apparitions of the Blessed Virgin on earth. That is why they are lasting so long and occurring so frequently."

2. The Blessed Virgin no longer appears to Mirjana Dragicevic. The last time she saw one of the daily apparitions was Christmas, 1982. Since then, the apparitions have ceased for her, except on her birthday (March 18, 1983). Mirjana knew that this latter would occur.

According to Mirjana, the Madonna confided the tenth and last secret to her during the apparition of December 25, 1982. She also disclosed the dates on which the different secrets will come to pass. The Blessed Virgin has revealed to Mirjana many things about the future, more than to any of the other youngsters so far. For that reason I am reporting below what Mirjana told me during our conversation on November 5, 1983. I am summarizing the substance of her account, without word-for-word quotations. Mirjana said:

Before the visible sign is given to humanity, there will be three warnings to the world. The warnings will be in the form of events on earth. Mirjana will be a witness to them. Three days before one of the admonitions, Mirjana will notify a priest of her choice. The witness of Mirjana will be a confirmation of the apparitions and a stimulus for the conversion of the world.

After the admonitions, the visible sign will appear at the site of the apparitions in Medjugorje for all the world to see. The sign will be given as a testimony to the apparitions and in order to call the people back to the faith.

The ninth and tenth secrets are serious. They concern chastisement for the sins of the world. Punishment is inevitable, for we cannot expect the whole world to be converted. The punishment can be diminished by prayer and penance, but it cannot be eliminated. Mirjana says that one of the evils that threatened the world, the one contained in the seventh secret, has been averted thanks to prayer and fasting. That is why the Blessed Virgin continues to encourage prayer and fasting: "You have forgotten that through prayer and fasting you can avert war and suspend the laws of nature."

After the first admonition, the others will follow in a rather short time. Thus, people will have some time for conversion.

The interval will be a period of grace and conversion. After the visible sign appears, those who are still alive will have little time for conversion. For that reason, the Blessed Virgin invites us to urgent conversion and reconciliation. The invitation to prayer and penance is meant to avert evil and war, but most of all to save souls.

According to Mirjana, the events predicted by the Blessed Virgin are near. By virtue of experience, Mirjana proclaims to the world: "Hurry, be converted; open your hearts to God."

In addition to this basic message, Mirjana related an apparition she had in 1982, which we believe sheds some light on some aspects of Church history. She spoke of an apparition in which Satan appeared to her disguised as the Blessed Virgin.[59] Satan asked Mirjana to renounce the Madonna and follow him. That way she could be happy in love and in life. He said that following the Virgin, on the contrary, would only lead to suffering. Mirjana rejected him, and immediately the Virgin arrived and Satan disappeared. Then the Blessed Virgin gave her the following message, in substance:

"Excuse me for this, but you must realize that Satan exists. One day he appeared before the throne of God and asked permission to submit the Church to a period of trial. God gave him permission to try the Church for one century. This century is under the power of the devil, but when the secrets confided to you come to pass, his power will be destroyed. Even now he is beginning to lose his power and has become aggressive. He is destroying marriages, creating divisions among priests, and is responsible for obsessions and murder. You must protect yourselves against these things through fasting and prayer, especially community prayer. Carry blessed objects with you. Put them in your house, and restore the use of holy water."

According to certain Catholic experts who have studied these apparitions,[60] this message of Mirjana may shed light on the vision Pope Leo XIII had. According to them, it was after having had an apocalyptic vision of the future of the Church that Leo XIII introduced the prayer to St. Michael which priests used to recite after Mass up to the time of the Second Vatican Council. These experts say that the century of trials foreseen by Leo XIII is about to end.

Holy Father, I do not want to be responsible for the ruin of anyone. I am doing my best. The world is being called to conversion and reconciliation. In writing to you, Holy Father, I am only doing my duty. After drafting this letter, I gave it to the visionaries, so that they might ask Our Blessed Virgin if the content was exact. Ivan Dragicevic related the following answer: "Yes, the contents of the letter are the truth. You must notify first the Supreme Pontiff and then the Bishop."

This letter is accompanied by fasting and prayers so that the Holy Spirit will guide your mind and your heart during this important moment in history.

Yours, in the Sacred Hearts of Jesus and Mary,
Fr. Tomislav Vlasic
Medjugorje,
December 2, 1983

Messages through Jelena Vasilj, "The Seventh Visionary"

Jelena Vasilj began reporting visions and messages of the Blessed Virgin Mary beginning on December 15, 1982. As previously mentioned, Jelena states that her experiences of Mary at present are by way of inner locutions, seeing and hearing Mary "with the heart", and not in the external apparitional manner reported by the other six visionaries. The messages transmitted by Jelena oftentimes serve the function of applying the principal messages given by Mary to the other six visionaries in the form of practical directives and counsels, to enable a living out of the messages in a personal, interior manner.

Messages transmitted by Jelena will be presented with as much chronological data as is available.

June 16, 1983: Jelena transmitted the following message concerning the existence of God and the role of Mary as the Queen of Peace: "I have come to tell the world: God is Truth, He exists. In Him is true happiness and abundance of life. I present myself here as Queen of Peace to tell the world that peace is necessary for the salvation of the world. In God is found true joy from which true peace flows."[61]

On the same day, Jelena reports this message regarding the Christian moral life: "Abandon yourself totally to God. Renounce disordered passions. Reject fear and give yourself—those who know how to abandon themselves will no longer know either obstacles or fear."[62]

June 26, 1983: Concerning the Christian response to enemies: "Love your enemies. Pray for them and bless them."[63]

June 28, 1983: A message for greater prayer and a specific call for prayer to the most Sacred Heart of Jesus: "Pray three hours a day . . . . You pray too little. Pray at least a half an hour morning and evening. Consecrate five minutes to the Sacred Heart; every family is its image."[64]

July 4, 1983: Mary calls for a greater quality of prayer and an openness to the Holy Spirit: "You have begun to pray three hours, but you look at your watches, preoccupied with your work. Be preoccupied with the one thing necessary, and let yourselves be guided by the Holy Spirit. Then your work will go well. Do not rush. Let your work be guided and you will see that everything will be accomplished well."[65]

Early July, 1983: Jelena conveys the following message warning of the danger and reality of the efforts of Satan: "Be alert. This is a dangerous time for you. The devil will try to turn you from this way. Those who give themselves to God will be the objects of attack."[66]

August 2, 1983: Mary requests a consecration to her Immaculate Heart, and a greater abandonment: "Consecrate yourselves to the Immaculate Heart. Abandon yourselves totally. I will protect you. I will pray to the Holy Spirit. Pray to Him yourselves."[67]*

August 15, 1983: On the Feast of the Assumption, Jelena transmits a message of Satan's anger: "Satan is enraged because of those who fast and are converted."[68]

August 25, 1983: Encouragement against temptation and towards peace of heart in the face of problems: "Do not be preoccupied. May peace reunite your hearts. The trouble comes only from Satan."[69]

September, 1983: Jelena conveyed these words to those of the prayer group returning to secular schools and environments: "Be alert not to diminish the spirit of prayer."[70]

October 20, 1983: Regarding the forming of a new youth prayer group, Mary asked for a four-year commitment, followed by these words: "This is not yet the moment to choose your vocation. The important thing is to first enter into prayer. Afterwards, you will make the right choice."[71]

Also on the same day, Jelena reported the call for a daily family consecration to the Most Sacred Heart of Jesus: "All families should consecrate themselves to the Sacred Heart every day. I would be very happy if the whole family were to come together for prayer every morning for a half an hour."[72]**

October 21, 1983: An emphasis on prayer to the Holy Spirit: "The important thing is to pray to the Holy Spirit that He may descend. When

---

* A prayer of consecration to the Immaculate Heart of Mary was dictated to Jelena and appears in Appendix I.

** A prayer of family consecration to the Sacred Heart of Jesus was dictated to Jelena, and appears in Appendix I.

you have Him, you have everything. People make a mistake when they turn only to the Saints to ask for something.''[73]

October 24, 1983: A message for the prayer group of which Jelena is a member: ''If you pray, a spring of life will flow from your hearts.''[74]

October 25, 1983: A further exhortation to prayer: ''Pray, pray, pray! Prayer will give you everything. It is through prayer that you can obtain everything.''[75]

October 27, 1983: A word on the strength of prayer and the futility of explanational discourse: ''Pray, pray, pray! You will never get anything from debate, but only from prayer. If you are questioned about me and about what I say, answer: 'Explanation is useless. Is it by praying that we understand best.' ''[76]

October 29, 1983: This message reflects the maternal endearment of Mary: ''I see that you are all tired. I want to take you all into my arms so that you can be with me.''[77]

October 29, 1983: Prayer is presented as the only means to authentic peace: ''Prayer is the only way that leads to peace. If you pray and fast, you will obtain all you ask.''[78]

October 30, 1983: A call for greater abandonment to Mary and evening prayer of thanksgiving to Christ: ''Why do you not give yourselves completely to me? I know that you pray a long time, but really hand yourselves over. Pray also in the evening when you have finished your day. Sit down in your room and say to Jesus, 'Thank you'. If in the evening you fall asleep in peace and praying, in the morning you will wake up thinking of Jesus and you will be able to ask Him for peace. But if you fall asleep distracted, in the morning you will be hazy, and you will forget even to pray.''[79]

November 5, 1983: A succinct call for perseverance: ''Be patient; be steadfast; keep praying.''[80]

November 8, 1983: This message speaks of the sinful state of the contemporary world, and the tepidity of faith in large numbers: ''Consider how sinful the world is today. . . . It appears to you not to sin because you are here in a peaceful world where there isn't disorder. But how many have tepid faith, and so do not listen to Jesus. If only you knew what I go through, you would never sin again. I need your prayers. Pray.''[81]

November 7, 1983: This dispatch conveys the great importance of sacramental Confession in the process of conversion: ''Don't go to Confession from habit to stay the same after it. No, that is not good. Confession should give drive to your faith. It should stir you, and draw you near to Jesus. If Confession doesn't mean much to you, you will be converted only with difficulty.''[82]

November 17, 1983: A request for the intensification of personal prayer that will pour out to others: "Pray. Don't look for a reason why I am constantly asking you to pray. Intensify (deepen) your personal prayer and let it spill over to others."[83]

November 18, 1983: A condemnation of local materialism: "In Medjugorje many people are intent on materialism from which they draw some profit, but they forget the one only good."[84]

November 29, 1983: This message conveys the maternity of Mary and the fraternity of Christ: "I am your good Mother, and Jesus is your great Friend. Fear nothing in His presence, but give Him your hearts. From the depth of your heart tell Him your sufferings. In this way, you will be revitalized in prayer, your heart set free, and in peace, without fear."[85]

December 4, 1983: A continual plea for greater prayer: "Pray. Pray. If you pray, I shall watch over you and be with you."[86]

December 15, 1983: Beginning on this day, Jelena also began receiving instructions concerning the topic of faith which she is recording for later disclosure.[87]

December 29, 1983: Mary desires a growth of interior peace and love through prayer: "I want a great peace, a great love, to grow in you. Then pray."[88]

Early January, 1984: At the beginning of the year 1984, Mary requested through Jelena that the parishioners come to church once during the week (preferably a day when there would be few pilgrims present) so that Mary could direct the spiritual life of the parish by way of weekly messages. Thursday was chosen by the parish priests, and beginning on the first Thursday in March, 1984, the six visionaries have reported specific messages for the parish during the Thursday evening apparitions (the messages of these Thursday appearances will be presented in the following section).[89]

January 8, 1984: A counsel to increase prayer, that will flower with the rebirth of Christ in the hearts: "Children, pray. I repeat: pray. I say it to you again. Don't think that Jesus is going to show Himself once again in the crib; but He is being reborn in your heart."[90]

January 18, 1984: Mary speaks of the reign of peace that arises from love of neighbor: "Pray. I wish to carve in each heart the sign of love. If you love every person, there is peace in you. If you are at peace with everyone, peace reigns."[91]

January 27, 1984: This message conveys specific directives for morning prayer, including prayer for the Pope, a prayer to the Holy Spirit, and the Rosary: "Pray and fast. I want you to draw your life from prayer . . . including each morning on waking, at least five Paters, Ave, Gloria, and a sixth for our Holy Father the Pope. Then the Creed and the prayer to the Holy Spirit. And, if it is possible, it would be good to say the Rosary."[92]

February 13, 1984: A change of heart through fasting, prayer, and self-offering: "Fast and pray. Give me your hearts. I want to change them completely. I want to refashion them. I want them to be pure."[93]

February 15, 1984: These words were received during a cold front with a chilling wind that prevented many people from attending evening Mass: "The wind is my symbol. I shall come in the wind. If the wind blows, know that I am with you. You have learned that the cross represents Christ. The cross which you have in your homes is a symbol of Him. My symbol is different."[94]

February 28, 1984: An endearing call to persevere in prayer and fasting: "Pray and fast. Know that I love you. I hold you on my knees."[95]

March 1, 1984: Jelena transmitted the directive to read the following section of the sixth chapter of the Gospel according to St. Matthew every Thursday:

> No one can serve two masters; for either he will hate the one and love the other, or he will be devoted to the one and despise the other. You cannot serve God and mammon.
>
> Therefore I tell you, do not be anxious about your life, what you should eat or what you shall drink, nor want about your body, what you shall put on. Is not life more than food, and the body more than clothing? Look at the birds of the air: they neither sow nor reap nor gather into barns, and yet your Heavenly Father feeds them. Are you not of more value than they? And which of you by being anxious can add one cubit to his span of life? And why are you anxious about your clothing? Consider the lilies in the field, how they grow; they neither toil nor spin; yet I tell you, even Solomon in all his glory was not arrayed like one of these. But if God so clothes the grass of the field, which today is alive and tomorrow is thrown into the oven, will he not much more clothe you, O men of little faith? Therefore, do not be anxious, saying, "What shall we eat?" or "What shall we drink?" or "What shall we wear?", for the Gentiles seek all these things; and your Heavenly Father knows that you need them all. But seek first his kingdom and his righteousness, and all these things shall be yours as well. Therefore, do not be anxious about tomorrow, for tomorrow will be anxious for itself. Let the day's own troubles be sufficient for the day (Matt. 6:24-34).[96]

Also on March 1, Jelena transmitted this message for a reduced type of sacrifice on Thursdays, the parish designated "Day of the Eucharist": "Let each one find their own way of fasting: the one who smokes should give up smoking, the one who drinks alcohol should not drink it; let each one give up some pleasure. Have these recommendations passed on to the parish."[97]

March 5, 1984: A message asking for a renewal in the Holy Spirit: "Pray and fast. Ask the Holy Spirit to renew your souls, to renew the whole world."[98]

March 14, 1984: This message comprises one of the few public messages transmitted through Marijana Vasilj, whose messages, also received through inner locutions, are usually only for her own personal spiritual direction: "Pray and fast that the reign of God may come among you. Let my Son inflame you with his fire (the Holy Spirit)."[99]

March 17, 1984: A reference to the parish novena in preparation for the Feast of the Annunciation: "Pray and fast so that during the novena, God will overwhelm you with His power."[100]

March 22, 1984: This message pertains to the achievement of an undisclosed aspect of Mary's plans: "Yesterday evening, I told you that one of the first wishes of my plan had been realized."[101]

March 27, 1984: An acknowledgement through Jelena that some members of the group have properly given themselves to God as previously requested: "In the group, some have given themselves to God to guide them. Let the will of God be done in you."[102]

March 30, 1984: This message transmitted by Jelena describes the profound gift of Christ received during the Mass, and the imperative to conscientiously attend the sacrifice of the Mass: "Children, I want the Holy Mass to be the gift of the day for you. Go to it; long for it to begin, because Jesus Himself gives Himself to you during the Mass. So, live for this moment when you are purified. Pray much that the Holy Spirit will renew your parish. If the people assist at Mass in a half-hearted fashion, they return home with cold, empty hearts."[103]

April 8, 1984: A further invocation for conversion through prayer: "I ask you to pray for the conversion of all. For this, I need prayer."[104]

Holy Week (April 15-April 22) 1984: Jelena received this message instructing the people to open their hearts to a special gift: "Raise your hands and open your hearts. Now, in the moment of the Resurrection, Jesus wants to give you a particular gift. This gift of my Son is my gift; it is this: you will undergo trials with great ease. We will be ready and will show you the way out if you will accept us. Do not say that the Holy Year[105] is now over and there is no more need to pray. On the contrary, reinforce your prayers, because the Holy Year is just one step forward."[106] After receiving these words, Jelena reported a vision of the risen Jesus. As light radiated from His wounds onto the people, Jelena said the risen Jesus spoke these words: "Receive my graces and tell the whole world there will be happiness only through me."[107]

April 19, (Holy Thursday), 1984: Mary conveyed to Jelena the following advice about spiritual preparation to offset trials and temptations: "I will tell you a spiritual secret: if you want to be stronger than evil, make an active conscience for yourself. That is, pray a reasonable amount in the morning, read a text of Holy Scripture, and plant the divine word in your heart, and try to live it during the day, especially in moments of trial, so you will be stronger than evil."[108]

May 23, 1984: Through Jelena, Mary expressed the desire for the parish to have a novena in preparation for the reception of the sacrament of Confirmation on the Feast of the Ascension (May 31, 1984).[109]

June 2, 1984: Through Jelena, Mary requested a novena in preparation for the Feast of Pentecost (June 10, 1984).[110]

Mid-June, 1984: Jelena reported that Mary asked for a preparation in prayer for the third anniversary of the beginning of the apparitions, and that the day, June 25, was to be celebrated as the "Feast of Mary, Queen of Peace."[111]

August, 1984: At the beginning of the month, Jelena transmitted a message intended for "the Pope and all Christians" establishing the exact date of her birthday as August 5. Her message requests a preparation for her two thousandth year birthday (August 5, 1984): "Throughout the centuries I have dedicated my entire life to you. Is it too much for you to dedicate three days for me? Do not do any work on that day but take your rosaries in your hands and pray."[112]

Mary specified fasting and prayer as the means of preparation for the feast of her birthday, and she predicted "great conversions" on that day.[113]

The following messages reported by Jelena are without specific chronological data, and fall into the general time between December 15, 1982, and November, 1984:

Concerning prayer in the family, Mary stated: "I know that every family can prayer four hours a day." Jelena responded: "But if I tell this to the people, they may back out." Mary replied: "Even you do not understand. It is only one sixth of the day." Jelena confirmed: "I know that you want us to pray continuously."[114]

In regard to the quality of prayer she is requesting, Mary stated: "When I say, 'Pray, pray, pray', I do not mean only increase the hours of prayer, but increase the desire to pray and to be in contact with God; to be in a continuous prayerful state of mind."[115]

Mary has indicated to Jelena that peace is needed for prayer. Peace should be present before prayer and during prayer, and that prayer should indeed conclude with peace and reflection.[116]

Regarding fear of anxiety over wars and chastisement, Jelena reported these words from Mary: "Do not think about wars, chastisements, evil. It is when you concentrate on these things that you are on the way to enter into them. Your responsibility is to accept divine peace, to live it."[117]

Directives concerning a peaceful, happy life: "If you want to be very happy, live a simple life, be humble, pray much, and do not worry about your problems; let them be settled by God."[118]

In response to the numerous questions presented by the visionaries, Mary has responded on several occasions. "Why so many questions?

The answer is in the Gospel.''[119]

Concerning the unavoidability of catastrophes, Jelena has conveyed these words: ''This comes from false prophets. They say 'On such a day at such a time there will be a catastrophe.' I have always said: 'The evil (the punishment) will come if the world is not converted!' Call people to conversion. Everything depends on your conversion.''[120]

At Jelena's request to know also the secrets revealed to the other six visionaries, Mary responded: ''Excuse me. That gift is for the others; it is not yours. What the six young people have said will happen. It is for you to believe like the rest.''[121]

At times of difficulties from others, Mary has said to Jelena: ''Do not defend yourself, but rather pray.''[122]

Finally, Jelena transmitted these words, calling for a ''blooming for Christ'' that will continue through the upcoming Christmas: ''I wish you to be a flower which will bloom for Jesus at Christmas—a flower which will not cease blooming when Christmas is over. I wish your hearts to be shepherds for Jesus.''[123]

Thursday Messages to the Parish
March, 1984 to March, 1985

As seen in the previous section, Jelena reported the desire of Mary to have the parish dedicate one day a week for spiritual and pastoral direction. This request was reported at the beginning of 1984, and the parish priests decided that Thursday would be designated as the requested day. Beginning in March, 1984, the six visionaries (usually through Marija) began receiving messages each Thursday, the content of which constitute a spiritual/pastoral guidance for the parish as a whole, and all others with an ''open heart''. The following are the Thursday messages from March 1, 1984, to March 7, 1985.[124]*

March 1, 1984: The first Thursday message reflects the desire of Mary to lead the parish in this unique way: ''Dear children! I have chosen this parish in a special way and I wish to lead it. I am watching over the parish with love and I wish them all to be mine. Thank you for your response this evening. I wish all of you always to be in great numbers with me and my Son. Every Thursday I will say a special message for you.''

March 8, 1984: A call for greater conversion: ''Thank you for your

* The Thursday messages are normally transmitted through Marija Pavlovic, though at instances Mary has spoken through one of the other visionaries. The Thursday Messages continue at present (March 1985).

response to my call! Dear children! Convert, you in the parish. That is my second wish. In that way all those who come here will be able to convert."

March 15, 1984: Mary requests a continual adoration of the Blessed Sacrament, stating that she is present with those who adore Jesus Christ in the Eucharist: "This evening, dear children, in a special way I am grateful to you for being here. Adore continually the most-holy Sacrament of the Altar. I am always present when the faithful are in adoration. Then special graces are being received."

March 22, 1984: At the beginning of Lent of 1984, Mary calls for devotion to the wounds of Jesus, and prayer to support her Son in His sufferings: "Dear children! This evening I am asking you in a special way during this Lent to honor the wounds of my Son, which He received from the sins of this parish. Unite with my prayers for this parish so that His sufferings may become bearable. Thank you for your response to my call. Endeavor to come, as many as possible."

March 29, 1984: Mary calls for an offering of sacrifices and a perseverance in trials, and to meditate on the continuing sufferings of God: "Dear children! This evening in a special way I am asking for your perseverance in trials. Ponder how the Almighty is still suffering, because of your sins.* So when the sufferings come, offer them as your sacrifice to God. Thank you for your response to my call."

April 5, 1984: This message requests devotion to the Sacred Heart of Jesus, and atonement for sins committed against His Divine Heart: "Dear children! This evening I am especially asking you to venerate the Heart of my Son, Jesus. Make an atonement for the wounds inflicted upon the Heart of my Son. That Heart has been offended with all sorts of sins. Thank you for your coming this evening."

April 12, 1984: A plea for unity and a reprimand about slandering within the parish: "Dear children! This evening I ask you to stop slandering and pray for the unity of the parish. For I and my Son have a special plan for this parish. Thank you for your response to my call."

April 19, 1984: A repeated call for prayer: "Dear children! Sympathize with me. Pray, pray, pray!"

April 26, 1984: This Thursday, the visionaries received no message from Mary. Marija concluded that Mary was only going to give the Thursday messages through Lent. Four days later, Marija asked Mary

---

* The Doctrine of the Mystical Body of Christ as it appears in the encyclical *Mystici Corporis* describes the mysterious way in which Christ, who suffered once and for all for the sins of humanity at Calvary, continues to suffer in some sense through His extension in the members of His body, the Church. St. Paul, in his letter to the Colossians, also discusses the mystery of man being able to "complete what is lacking in the sufferings of Christ" (Col. 1:24).

during the daily apparition the following question: "Dear Madonna, why have you not given me the message to the parish on [last] Thursday?" Our Lady replied: "I do not wish to force anyone to anything he doesn't feel and doesn't wish, even though I had special messages for the parish to awaken the faith of every believer. But only a small number has accepted the messages on Thursdays. At the beginning there were more of them. But now it looks as if it had become something ordinary to them. And now some have been asking recently for the message out of their curiosity and not out of their faith and devotion to my Son and me."

May 10, 1984: The parish was concerned that Mary would no longer give specific Thursday messages for them. The following Thursday Mary gave the following message: "I am still speaking to you and I intend to continue so. Only listen to my instructions."

May 17, 1984: The visionaries report Mary's joy at their devotion to her: "Dear Children! Today I am very happy because there are many of those who desire to devote themselves to me. I thank you! You have not been mistaken. My Son Jesus Christ wishes to bestow on you special graces through me. My Son is happy because of your dedication. Thank you, because you have responded to my call."

May 24, 1984: Mary emphasizes her maternal love that continues even without a response of love: "Dear children! I have told you already that I have chosen you in a special way, the way you are. I, your Mother, love you all. And in any moment when it is difficult for you, don't be afraid. I love you even when you are far from me and my Son. I ask you not to allow my heart to cry with blood because of the souls which get lost in sin. Therefore, dear children, pray, pray, pray! Thank you for your response to my call."

May 31, 1984: This Thursday was the feast of the Ascension. There were many pilgrims present at St. James Church, and that evening Mary offered no message. But Marija reported Mary saying that she would give the parish a message on Saturday, to be announced on Sunday.

June 2, 1984: On Saturday, the first day of the novena to prepare for Pentecost (as called for through Jelena), Mary calls for prayer to enable the outpouring of the Holy Spirit upon the parish and all families: "Dear children! This evening I wish to say: in the days of this novena, pray for the outpouring of the Holy Spirit upon all your families and your parish. Pray, and you shall not regret it. God shall give you the gifts and you shall glorify Him for it until the end of your life. Thank you for your response to my call."

June 9, 1984: On the eve of Pentecost, the visionaries reported a message directing the parish to pray for the Spirit of Truth in order to convey these messages without any additions or deletions along with the call for greater prayer: "Dear children! Tomorrow night [Pentecost] pray for the Spirit of Truth. Especially you from the parish. You need the Spirit of Truth in order to be able to convey the messages the way they are, without adding to them or taking away anything: the way I gave them to you. Pray that the Holy Spirit may inspire you with the spirit of prayer, that you pray more. I, as your Mother, say that you pray little. Thank you for your response to my call.''

June 14, 1984: No special message was given, nor any publicly known reason for its absence.

June 21, 1984: Another exhortation to prayer: "Pray, pray, pray! Thank you for your response to my call.''

July 5, 1984: A directive to work less, pray more, and to find true rest in prayer: "Dear children! Today I wish to tell you: pray before your every work and end your work with prayer. If you do that, God will bless you and your work. These days you have been praying too little and working too much. Pray therefore. In prayer you will find rest. Thank you for your response to my call.''

July 12, 1984: Mary restates the reality of the efforts of Satan to defeat her plans at Medjugorje. She promises her own prayers to Christ for the peoples' experiencing of the victory of Jesus: "Dear children! These days Satan is trying to thwart all my plans. Pray that his plan may not be fulfilled. I will pray to my Son Jesus to give you the grace that you may in Satan's temptations experience the victory of Jesus. Thank you for your response to my call.''

July 19, 1984: Strength against temptations, and a reassurance of Mary's presence with the parish during times of temptation: "Dear children! These days you have been experiencing how Satan is working. I am always watching over you. And I have given myself up to you and I sympathize with you even in the smallest temptations. Thank you for your response to my call.''

July 26, 1984: Mary entreats persistent prayer and penance, particularly from the youth of the parish: "Dear children! Today also I would like to call you to a persistent prayer and penance. Especially let the young people of this parish be more active in their prayers. Thank you for your response to my call.''

August 2, 1984: Greater prayer for the conversion of sinners: "Dear children! Today I am happy and I thank you for your prayers. Pray more these days for the conversion of sinners. Thank you for your response to my call.''

August 11, 1984: This message asks for continual prayer to offset the efforts of Satan and for an abandonment to Christ: "Dear children! Pray, because Satan is continually trying to thwart my plans. Pray with your heart and in prayer give yourselves up to Jesus.''

August 14, 1984: (Eve of the Feast of the Assumption): This was an unexpected apparition which transmitted a message to Ivan during prayer at home before going to Church for the evening service. He was told to relay the follow message calling for Wednesday and Friday fasts and the full Rosary daily: "I ask the people to pray with me these days. Pray all the more. Fast strictly on Wednesday and Friday; say every day at least one Rosary: Joyful, Sorrowful, and Glorious Mysteries." Mary asked the parish and the people of surrounding areas especially to accept this message with a resolute will.

August 16, 1984: This message requests the living out of her messages and the spreading of their contents: "Dear children! I ask you, especially you from the parish, to live according to my messages and relate them to others, whomever you meet. Thank you for your response to my call."

August 23, 1984: "Pray, pray, pray!" This cry for perseverance in prayer was presented along with a request for the people, and especially the young, to keep order in the church during the Mass.

August 30, 1984: Mary makes reference in this message to the cross on the mountain erected in 1933, in commemoration of the nineteen hundredth anniversary of Calvary. She calls for prayers at the foot of the cross: "Dear children! The cross had been in God's plan when you built it. These days especially go on the mountain and pray at the foot of the cross. I need your prayers. Thank you for your response to my call."

September 6, 1984: Mary asks for prayers at the foot of the cross: "Dear children! Without prayer there is no peace. Therefore I say to you, dear children, pray at the foot of the cross for peace. Thank you for your response to my call."

September 13, 1984: The call is made for prayer to counter the ubiquitous sins of the world: "Dear children! I continually need your prayer. You wonder what all these prayers are for. Turn around, dear children, and you will see how much ground sin has gained in this world. Therefore, pray that Jesus may win. Thank you for your response to my call."

September 20, 1984: Mary requests a fasting, not out of convention but from the heart, out of gratitude for her lengthy visit: "Dear children! Today I ask you to start fasting from your heart. There are many people who fast, but only because everyone else is fasting. It has become a custom which no one wants to stop. I ask the parish to fast out of gratitude to God for having let me remain this long in this parish. Dear children, fast and pray with your heart. Thank you for your response to my call."

September 27, 1984: The Family Rosary is asked for in this message: "Dear children! You have helped with your prayers for my plans to be fulfilled. Pray continually that they may be fulfilled to the full. I ask the families of the parish to recite the Family Rosary. Thank you for your response to my call."

October 4, 1984: A call for the entire parish to pray, to allow Mary to offer all their prayers and sufferings to God: "Dear children! Today I would like to tell you that your prayers delight me, but there are those in the parish who do not pray and my heart is sad. Pray therefore that I may bring all your sufferings and prayers to the Lord. Thank you for your response to my call."

October 8, 1984: This message was not delivered in the church, but was received by Jakov at his house. Because of an illness, Jakov did not go to the church on this day. The message calls for an evening Rosary every night for the conversion of sinners: "Dear children! Let all the prayers which you say in your houses in the evening be for the conversion of sinners, because the world is in great sin. Pray the Rosary every evening."

October 11, 1984: Mary gives thanks to the people for the offering of their trials to God, and calls the parish to continue presenting their burdens to God (the "testing" referred to concerns a long rain in the middle of the local harvest season which caused great ruin to the crop harvest): "Dear children! Thank you for offering all your pains to God, even now when He is testing you through the fruits which you are reaping. Be aware, dear children, that He loves you and for that reason He tests you. Always present your burdens to God and do not worry. Thank you for your response to my call."

October 18, 1984: The visionaries transmitted the following words requesting a daily reading of Sacred Scripture, and its location in a visible, accessible place in the house: "Dear children! Today I ask you to read the Bible in your houses every day and let it be on a visible place in the house so that it always encourages you to read it and pray. Thank you for your response to my call."

October 25, 1984: Mary directs the parish to pray for the graces of God especially during this month: "Dear children! Pray during this month. God gave me this month. I give it to you. Pray and ask for the graces of God. I will pray that He gives them to you. Thank you for your response to my call."

November 1, 1984: Mary calls for a renewal of family prayer, and that prayer take first place in the priorities of each family: "Dear children! Today I call you to the renewal of family prayer in your homes. The field work is over. Now you all devote yourselves to prayer. Let prayer take the first place in your families. Thank you for your response to my call."

November 8, 1984: A petition to pray to the Holy Spirit for enlightenment to see the abundance of graces being offered: "Dear children! You are not aware of the messages which God is sending to you through me. He is giving you great graces and you are not grasping them. Pray to the Holy Spirit for enlightenment—if you only knew how great are the graces

God is giving you, you would pray without ceasing. Thank you for your response to my call.''

November 15, 1984: This message brings a counsel to pray, so as to come to know the love of God and the love of Mary: "Dear children! You are a chosen people and God gave you great graces. You are not aware of every message I am giving you. Now I only wish to tell you, 'pray, pray, pray!' I do not know what else to tell you because I love you and wish that you, in prayer, would come to know my love and the love of God. Thank you for your response to my call.''

November 22, 1984: This message comes at the transition from Ordinary time to Advent, the beginning of the liturgical year of the Church, and calls for a living of the main messages from the heart: "Dear children! These days live all the messages and keep rooting them in your hearts until Thursday. Thank you for your response to my call.''

November 29, 1984: This profound message instructs the people to do all things out of love, to recognize Mary's maternal mission on earth, and to carry the cross, but not by force, leading to the glorification of God: "Dear children! You do not know how to love, and you do not know how to listen with love to the words I give you. Be aware, my beloved ones, that I am your Mother and that I am coming upon earth to teach you to listen out of love and to pray out of love, and to carry your cross, but not by force. Through the cross, God is glorified in every man. Thank you for your response to my call.''

December 6, 1984: Mary asks for more family prayer as preparation for an unforgettable Christmas, and a more heartfelt acceptance of her messages: "Dear children! These days I am calling you to family prayer. In God's name, many times I have given you messages, but you will not listen. This Christmas will be unforgettable for you if you will only accept the messages I am giving you. Dear children, do not allow that day of joy to be a day of greatest sorrow for me.''

December 13, 1984: A lesson of love, starting with family and extending to the parish, and then to all pilgrims: "Dear children! You know that the day of joy is coming near, but without love you cannot succeed in doing anything. Therefore begin first by loving your own family, everyone in the parish, and then you will be able to love and accept all those who are coming here. This week must be the week in which you must learn how to love. Thank you for responding to my call.''

December 20, 1984: Mary asks for a concrete sign of every parish family's abandonment to Jesus: "Today I wish you to do something concrete for Jesus. I desire that every family of the parish offer a flower for the day of joy, as a sign of their abandonment to Jesus. I desire that every member of the family has a flower near the crib [manger in the

Church] so that Jesus may come and see your devotion to Him. Thank you!''

December 27, 1984: This messages speaks of the triumph of God over Satan in the hearts of the people on Christmas: "Dear children! This Christmas Satan wanted in a special way to thwart God's plans. But you, dear children, have recognized him on the day of Christmas. God overcame him in all your hearts. Let your heart then be filled continuously with joy. Thank you for responding to my call.''

January 3, 1985: On the first Thursday of the new year, Mary calls for thanksgiving for the many graces received: "Dear children! In these days God has granted you many precious graces. Let this week be a week of thanksgiving for the graces God has granted you. Thank you for responding to my call.''

January 10, 1985: A message of thanks for the faithful believers in the parish: "Dear children! Today I want to thank you for all your sacrifices, and I especially thank those who have become dear to my heart and come here gladly. There are many parishioners who are not listening to the messages. But because of those who are in a special way close to my heart, because of them, I give messages to the parish. And I will continue giving them for I love you, and wish you to spread them by your hearts. Thank you for responding to my call.''

January 17, 1985: A call to persevere in prayer, in spite of temptations by Satan to stop: "In these days Satan is fighting deviously against the parish, and you, dear children, are asleep in prayer, and only some are going to Mass. Persevere in these days of temptations. Thank you for responding to my call.''

January 24, 1985: Mary praises the parish for its renewal in prayer, and reinforces the disarming power of prayer against the violence of Satan: "Dear children! These days you have savored the sweetness of God through the renewal in your parish. Satan is working even more violently to take away the joy from each one of you. Through prayer you can totally disarm him and ensure happiness. Thank you for responding to my call.''

January 31, 1985: A call to open our hearts to the abundant graces from the Father: "Dear children! Today I wish to tell you to open your hearts to God, like flowers in Spring yearning for the sun. I am your Mother, and I always want you to be closer to the Father, and that He will always give abundant gifts to your hearts. Thank you for responding to my call.''

February 7, 1985 A warning against the efforts by Satan in the parish: "Dear children! Satan is manifesting himself in this parish in a particular way, these days. Pray, dear children, that God's plan is carried out, and that every work of Satan is turned to the glory of God. I have remained this long to help you in your great trials. Thank you for responding to my call.''

February 14, 1985: A call for perseverance in living out the message, and for the reading of Scripture in the family: ''Dear children! Today is the day when I give you the message for the parish, but the whole parish is not accepting the messages and does not live them. I am sad, and I wish you, dear children, to listen to me and to live my messages. Every family must pray family prayer and read the Bible. Thank you for responding to my call.''

February 21, 1985: A strong request for a more faithful answer to Mary's call: ''Dear children! From day to day I have been appealing to you for renewal and prayer in the parish. But you are not accepting. Today, I am appealing to you for the last time. This is the season of Lent, and you as a parish in Lent can be moved, for the sake of love, to my call. If you do not do that, I do not wish to give you messages that God has permitted me. Thank you for responding to my call.''

February 28, 1985: The power of love and abandonment to God: ''Dear children! Today I call you to live the word this week. I love God. Dear children! With love you will achieve everything, and even what you think is impossible. God wants this parish to belong to Him completely. And I want that too. Thank you for responding to my call.''

March 7, 1985: A call for renewed family prayer and Mass attendance: ''Dear children! Today I invite you to renew prayer in your families. Dear children, encourage the very young to pray and to go to Holy Mass. Thank you for your response to my call.''

Messages Reported Between June, 1984
and December, 1984
Without Specific Chronological Data

The following messages are without specific chronological data, but have occurred within the approximate time frame of June, 1984 to January, 1985. The contents of the messages seem to emphasize the profound love of God and Mary for the people, the desire of Mary to have more people open their hearts to her, and the continual imperative to pray:[125]

Dear children! If you only knew how great my love is for you, you would cry for joy.

Dear children! When someone is standing before you asking a favor of you, respond by giving. I stand before many hearts and they do not open to me. Pray that the world may receive my love.

Dear children! I love you so much, and when you love me, you can feel it. I bless you in the name of the Holy Trinity and in my name. Stay in peace.

Dear children! The love of God has not flowed over the whole world. Pray, therefore.

Dear children! I desire the whole world to become my children, but they are not willing. I want to give them everything. Pray, therefore.

This concludes the presentation of the messages in their raw form as reported by the six visionaries and Jelena Vasilj, the seventh visionary. Again, all the preceding messages were approved by the parish priests of St. James Church as messages reported by the seven youths. Let us now proceed to a doctrinal and thematic synthesis of these messages attributed by the youths to the "Queen of Peace".

Notes
Chapter One

[1] Account of the "Message of Medjugorje" by Father Tomislav Vlasic, O.F.M., August 15, 1983, as it appears in *Our Lady, Queen of Peace*, pamphlet published by Peter Batty, East Sussex, England, 1984, p. 10.

[2] *Ibid.*

[3] *Ibid.*

[4] *Ibid.*

[5] Svetozar Kraljevic, O.F.M., *Apparitions of Our Lady of Medjugorje*, original English manuscript, Diocese of Mostar, Yugoslavia, p. 8. The original manuscript has been edited by Michael Scanlan, T.O.R., and published under the same title by the Franciscan Herald Press, Chicago, 1984.

[6] Interview of Vicka Ivankovic and Fr. Tomislav Vlasic, O.F.M., March 15, 1982, as recorded by Fr. Kraljevic in original manuscript. Note: This personal message is included because of its significance as the first words received by the children.

[7] *Ibid.*

[8] *Ibid.*, p. 11.

[9] *Ibid.*

[10] *Ibid.*

[11] *Ibid.*

[12] René Laurentin and Ljudevit Rupcic, *Is the Virgin Mary Appearing at Medjugorje?*, The Word Among Us Press, Washington, 1984, p. 79.

[13] Kraljevic, original manuscript, p. 15.

[14] *Ibid.*

[15] *Ibid.*

[16] *Ibid.*

[17] *Ibid.*

[18] *Ibid.*

[19] *Ibid.*

[20] Laurentin, *Is the Virgin Mary Appearing?*, p. 79. Note: There seems to have been some local tradition of reciting the Our Father, Hail Mary, and Glory Be seven times, but the reciting of the Creed was certainly added by Mary.

[21] This entire conversation was taped by Grgo Kozina, a local townsperson present at the site of the apparition. The transcript of the tape appears in the original manuscript of Fr. Kraljevic, p. 23.

[22] Interview of Fr. Jozo Zovko, at that time pastor of St. James Parish, with five of the six children (Ivan was not present), as recorded in Fr. Kraljevic, original manuscript, p. 23. Note: The children asked Mary if she would begin appearing inside the church when the local Communist authorities forbad any continued religious gathering outside the Church.

[23] Kraljevic, original manuscript, p. 25.

[24] *Ibid.*

[25] *Ibid.*

[26] *Ibid.*

[27] *Ibid.*, p. 31.

[28] *Ibid.*, p. 31.

[29] *Ibid.*

[30] *Ibid.*

[31] Lucy Rooney, S.N.D. and Robert Faricy, S.J., *Mary, Queen of Peace*, Fowler Wright Books, Ltd., Great Britain, 1984, p. 39.

[32] Kraljevic, original manuscript, p. 39.

[33] *Ibid.*

[34] *Ibid.*

[35] Rooney, *Queen of Peace*, p. 36.

[36] Kraljevic, original manuscript, p. 39.

[37] Rooney, *Queen of Peace*, p. 39.

[38] Laurentin, *Is the Virgin Appearing?*, p. 80. Note: This may be a reference to those unbelievers with "a hardened heart", where even the sign will not be great enough impetus for conversion. In a similar message as described by Fr. Tomislav Vlasic, the sentence reads, "When the sign comes it will be too late for many (pamphlet, *Our Lady, Queen of Peace*, published by Peter Batty, East Sussex, England, p. 10.).

[39] *Ibid.*, p. 81.

[40] *Ibid.*

[41] Kraljevic, original manuscript, p. 36.

[42] *Ibid.* Note: From the manuscript it appears that this is an editorial combination of Mary's responses to petitions of healing, rather than just one quote.

[43] *Ibid.*

[44] *Ibid.*, p. 39.

[45] *Ibid.*

[46] *Ibid.*

[47] *Ibid.* Note: Quotation marks are not included because it is not clear whether this is a summary of content or a specific message.

[48] *Ibid.*

[49] Kraljevic, original manuscript, p. 70.

[50] *Ibid.*

[51] Rooney, *Queen of Peace*, p. 39.

[52] *Ibid.*, p. 38.

[53] *Ibid.*, p. 36.

[54] *Ibid.*, p. 25.

[55] Laurentin, *Is the Virgin Mary Appearing?*, p. 120. Note: This scripture passage is found in the Gospel of John 2:4.

[56] "Interview with Mirjana Dragicevic" in Kraljevic, original manuscript, p. 80.

[57] This is a reference to the partially revealed secrets from Fatima.

[58] *Report Sent to Rome by the Parish of Medjugorje*, original manuscript from St. James Parish, Medjugorje. The same report can be found in Laurentin, *Is the Virgin Mary Appearing?*, Appendix 1, p. 142.

[59] The description of the appearance of Satan disguised as Mary is not found in Mirjana's earlier account of the experience in her interview with Fr. Vlasic.

[60] There are no names offered in this reference to Catholic experts.

[61] Laurentin, *Is the Virgin Appearing?*, p. 80.

[62] *Ibid.*

[63] *Ibid.*

[64] *Ibid.*

[65] *Ibid.*

[66] *Ibid.*

[67] *Ibid.*

[68] *Ibid.*

[69] *Ibid.*

[70] *Ibid.*

[71] *Ibid.*

[72] *Ibid.*

[73] *Ibid.*

[74] Laurentin, *Dernieres Nouvelles*, ed., O.E.I.L., translated from the French, 1984, p. 33.

[75] *Ibid.*

[76] *Ibid.*

[77] *Ibid.*

[78] *Ibid.*

[79] *Ibid.*

[80] *Ibid.*

[81] *Ibid.*, p. 34.

[82] *Ibid.*

[83] *Ibid.*

[84] *Ibid.*

[85] *Ibid.*

[86] *Ibid.*

[87] Laurentin, *Is the Virgin Mary Appearing?*, p. 80.

[88] Laurentin, *Dernieres*, p. 34.

[89] *Thursday Messages to the Parish of Medjugorje*, obtained from St. James Parish Rectory, Medjugorje, Yugoslavia.

[90] Laurentin, *Dernieres*, p. 35.

[91] *Ibid.*

[92] *Ibid.*

[93] *Ibid.*

[94] *Ibid.*

[95] *Ibid.*

[96] *Thursday Messages*, St. James Parish Rectory, Medjugorje.

[97] Laurentin, *Dernieres*, p. 36.

[98] *Ibid.*

[99] *Ibid.*

[100] *Ibid.*

[101] *Ibid.*

[102] *Ibid.*, p. 42.

[103] *Ibid.*

[104] *Ibid.*

[105] Easter Sunday, April 22, 1984, was the formal closing of the 1983 Holy Year called by Pope John Paul II.

[106] Rooney, *Queen of Peace*, p. 78.

[107] *Ibid.*

[108] *Ibid.*

[109] *Messages from Jelena Vasilj*, obtained from St. James Parish Rectory, Medjugorje, Yugoslavia.

[110] *Ibid.*

[111] Mary was questioned as to why June 25 was chosen instead of June 24, the actual first day of the apparitions. Mary responded by saying that the first day was the day the

children ran away. Kraljevic, original manuscript, p. 28.

[112] *Messages from Jelena Vasilj*, St. James Parish Rectory, Medjugorje, Yugoslavia.

[113] Rooney, *Queen of Peace*, p. 77.

[114] *Ibid.*, p. 79.

[115] *Ibid.*, p. 77.

[116] *Ibid.*, p. 79.

[117] *Ibid.*

[118] *Ibid.*

[119] Laurentin, *Is the Virgin Mary Appearing?*, p. 73.

[120] *Ibid.*, p. 82.

[121] *Ibid.*, p. 75.

[122] *Ibid.*

[123] *Messages from Jelena*, St. James Parish.

[124] *Thursday Rectory Messages to the Parish of Medjugorje*, obtained from St. James Parish, Medjugorje.

[125] *Recent Messages*, obtained from St. James Parish Rectory, Medjugorje, Yugoslavia.

CHAPTER TWO

Doctrinal and Thematic Synthesis of the Medjugorje Message

The messages reported by the six visionaries and Jelena, the seventh visionary, have been categorized by the author into general doctrinal and thematic divisions according to the subject-matter of the respective messages. These themes do not exhaust the content of the individual messages, but rather provide a doctrinal and thematic synthesis of that content.

The messages are further grouped into "foundational" themes and "developmental" themes. The foundational themes are those groups of messages that comprise the basis for the entire message of Medjugorje, the topical pillars upon which all the individual messages rest. The developmental themes are those content categories which flow from the foundational themes, and generally serve the purpose of specifying, concretizing, and implementing the content found in the foundational themes. But the division of the content into "foundational" and "developmental" is in no way to suggest that the developmental content is to be seen as in any sense inferior to the foundational content; nor does it imply that the developmental content in some sense fails to call for the same degree of acceptance and incorporation as does the content found in the foundational categories. These divisions have been made by the author for the purpose of synthesizing the doctrinal and thematic content of the Medjugorjian message, and neither to prioritize doctrinally nor to substitute for the full content of the messages reported by the visionaries.

A. Medjugorje Foundational Themes

1. Faith

The call to believe and its response in faith is an essential prerequisite that surfaces from the content of the messages. What type of faith are the reported messages calling for? René Laurentin answers that question as follows:

Our Lady strongly insists on the need for a living faith, the kind of faith Jesus required. It is a faith which concentrates on God, but which knows the power of God to bring about the healing, both interior and exterior, both personal and social.[1]

The call to faith appears as a crucial request from the beginning of the apparitions. On the sixth day of the reported appearances, faith in the one God is requested by Mary from all the people present:

Visionaries: Dear Madonna! What do you wish from these people?
Mary: There is one God and one faith. Believe firmly.[2]

In the interview with Mirjana, faith constitutes the first spiritual directive specified by Mary: "She always recommended faith, prayer, and fasting."[3] Mary has also spoken of the necessity of prayer to sustain a living faith: "Faith cannot be alive without prayer."[4]

There also seems to be a proximate call to faith in the authenticity of the apparitions. On June 26, 1981, the third day of the apparitions, the visionaries asked Mary for a specific message for priests. Mary responded: "Let the priests firmly believe." And to the request of Vicka for a miracle that would prove the authenticity of Mary's appearances to the others, Mary stated: "Let those who do not see believe as if they see."[5]

Both a general call to a more resolute faith in the one true God, and a proximate call to faith in the apparitions themselves comprise the principal Medjugorjian call to faith.

2. Prayer

The messages have emphatically called for prayer, both in greater quantity and intensity, establishing prayer as the principal means of attaining the peace of Christ. Several of the Thursday messages to the parish have been nothing but a repeated request for prayer, as was this message on April 19, 1984: "Dear children! Sympathize with me. Pray, pray, pray!"[6] A later Thursday message asked for a decrease in work and an increase in prayer: "These days you have been praying too little and working too much. Pray, therefore. In prayer you will find rest."[7]

Through Jelena, Mary has specified the call to prayer, both in amount and in degree: "Pray three hours a day. . . .* You pray too little. Pray at least half an hour morning and evening.";[8] and further: "When I say, 'Pray, pray, pray,' I do not mean only to increase the hours of prayer, but increase the desire to pray and to be in contact with God; to be in a continuous prayerful state of mind."[9] It is only through the crucial mandate to consistent prayer, according to the messages, that the peace and salvation of Christ can be attained by those who believe.

* This message was specifically directed to a youth prayer group in Medjugorje. Whether this comprises a universal call or not, the message clearly reinforces the general call to a *greater generosity* of prayer than ever before.

3. Fasting

A return to the practice of fasting is a clear directive in the message content. Mary has made known her concern about the discarding of this powerful spiritual discipline, stating: "Christians have forgotten they can prevent war and even natural calamities by prayer and fasting."[10]

During an unexpected appearance to Ivan on August 14, 1984, Mary requested a strict fast twice a week: "Fast strictly on Wednesdays and Fridays."[11] Near the beginning of the apparitions, the youths asked Mary what was the best fast, to which she replied: "A fast of bread and water."[12]

And in regard to the quality of the fasting, this Thursday message was reported by Marija on September 20, 1984:

> Dear children! Today I ask you to start fasting from the heart! There are many people who fast, but only because everyone else is fasting. It has become a custom which no one wants to stop. I ask the parish to fast out of gratitude to God for having let me remain this long in the parish. Dear children, fast and pray with your hearts.[13]

4. Penance

The general call to penance, that form of self-denial for the sake of Christ (of which fasting is a major constituent), also presents itself as a fundamental theme. A little over a month after the beginning of the apparitions, the visionaries were asked by Mary to climb to the top of the mountain of the cross at approximately two o'clock in the morning to pray that people will do penance for the conversion of sinners.[14]

The same call to penance continues almost three years later, when Mary requests the continuation of penance during this Thursday message of July 26, 1984: "Dear children! Today I would like to call you to a persistent prayer *and penance*. . . ."[15]

In the interview with Mirjana, the question is raised if any specific message has been given for priests and bishops, to which Mirjana answered: "No, but a long time ago she said that they should accept us, help us as much as they can, and pray more and *do penance*."[16]

And the report sent to Pope John Paul II by Fr. Tomislav Vlasic and the visionaries presents the ultimate goal of both penance and prayer to be the salvation of souls: "The invitation to prayer *and penance* is meant to avert evil and war, but most of all to save souls."[17]

5. Conversion

The call to convert is a call to everyone, both believers and unbelievers. For believers, the call to conversion prescribes a greater turning of one's heart to God, away from sin, and a deepening of faith in contrition for sin; for the unbeliever, it is the call to accept the one true God in faith, and to be converted from the sinfulness of the world through repentence. Mary's emphatic plea for conversion is accompanied by an accentuated urgency:

> Hasten your conversion. Do not wait for the sign that has been announced for the unbelievers; it will already be too late for them to have a conversion. You who believe, be converted, and deepen your faith.[18]

The same immediacy can be found in the summary Mirjana makes of Mary's call to convert: "I say to all people, 'Convert'—the same as she did. 'Convert while there's still time.' "[19]

A message reported by the visionaries in April, 1983 represents a world-wide request for conversion:

> The only word I wish to speak is for the conversion of the whole world. I wish to speak it to the whole world. I ask nothing but conversion. . . . It is my desire. . . . Be converted. . . . Leave everything; that comes from conversion.[20]

Because of the fundamental imperative for the conversion of sinners, Mary has requested in her Thursday message to the parish a greater increase of prayer for its cause: "Pray these days for the conversion of sinners" (August 2, 1984);[21] and further: "Let all the prayers which you say in your houses in the evenings be for the conversion of sinners, because the world is in great sin" (October 8, 1984).[22]

6. Peace

> Peace, peace, peace . . . nothing but peace. Men must be reconciled with God and with each other. For this to happen, it is necessary to believe, to pray, to fast, and to go to Confession. Go in God's peace.[23]

This message from the third day of the apparitions, June 26, 1981, is a profound synthesis of the call to peace, vitally present in the message of Medjugorje. Peace is posed as the all-encompassing goal, and it is a peace that comes firstly when men reconcile themselves with God, and then bearing fruition in a peaceful reconciliation between humanity. Peace is attainable only through conversion, achieved through faith, prayer, fasting, penance, and the other means offered by Mary for acquiring the interior peace of Christ.

The nature of the peace present in the message points primarily to an interior peace, a divine peace of soul. This is clear in the statements of Mirjana regarding Mary's message of peace:

> *Fr. Vlasic:*   So the message of the Madonna is a message of peace?
> *Mirjana:*   Yes. Primarily peace of soul. If a person has it in his soul, he is surrounded by it.[24]

The same emphasis on the divine peace of soul, as a clear priority over fears and anxieties stemming from news of an upcoming world punishment, surfaces in this message transmitted through Jelena, received when Jelena had in fact become anxious over thoughts of world chastisement:

> Do not think about wars, chastisements, evil. It is when you concentrate on these things that you are on the way to enter into them. Your responsibility is to accept divine peace; to live it.[25]

But the call to the inner peace of Christ must also bear fruit in a reconciliation for humanity, a social peace based on a spiritual peace. It is for this reason that the practice of prayer plays such an integral role in the call for peace, as evident in the Thursday message to the parish on September 6, 1984: "Dear children! Without prayer, there is no *peace*. Therefore I say to you, dear children, pray at the foot of the cross *for peace*."[26]

So central and crucial is the call to peace in the message of Medjugorje that the visionaries have reported Mary to have identified herself early in the apparitions precisely as the "Queen of Peace".[27]

B. Medjugorje Developmental Themes

1. Jesus Christ—The One Redeemer and Mediator

The content of the messages uniformly points to Jesus Christ as the single redeemer of humanity and to His sole role as the mediator for all people to the heavenly Father. The Christological focus of the messages is central, whether it be a request for a greater devotion "to my Son", prayer for the "victory of Jesus", or atonement made for offenses committed against the "Heart of my Son". The attestation to Christ as the sole source of salvation is clear in a message transmitted in early January, 1982: "My Son suffered on the cross. He redeemed the world on the cross. Salvation comes from the cross."[28] And the declaration of Christ as the sole mediator for all peoples appears in the following passage: "In God's eyes, there are no divisions and no religions. You in the world have made the divisions. The one mediator is Jesus Christ."[29]

The messages reflect a determinative effort on the part of Mary to focus the direction of both prayer and the orientation of believers in general to her Son: "Please pray to Jesus. I am His Mother and I intercede for you to Him. But all prayers go to Jesus."[30] And when Mary has appeared on several occasions with Jesus, either as a child or in His Passion, she has stated: "Do whatever He tells you."[31]

2. Renewal in the Holy Spirit

An emphasis on a return to prayer and guidance by the often-times forgotten Third Person of the Trinity is also accentuated in the content. In a message transmitted by Jelena, prayer and a turning to the Holy Spirit is the focal directive:

> The important thing is to pray to the Holy Spirit that He may descend. When you have Him, you have everything. People make a mistake when they turn only to the Saints for everything.[32]

Mary called for a novena to the Holy Spirit in preparation for Pentecost in June, 1984, and in this Thursday message to the parish received during the novena, she requested prayer for the outpouring of the Paraclete: "In the days of this novena, pray for the outpouring of the Holy Spirit upon all your families and your parish."[33]

On the eve of Pentecost, Mary invoked prayer to the "Spirit of Truth" so as to assist them in their prayer, and in conveying the transmitted messages without any additions or subtractions:

> Pray to the Spirit of Truth. Especially you from the parish. You need the Spirit of Truth in order to convey the messages the way they are, without adding to them or taking away anything; the way I gave them to you. Pray that the Holy Spirit may inspire you with the spirit of prayer.[34]

Two other messages transmitted through Jelena in July and August of 1983 instruct the people to allow the Holy Spirit to guide them, and to increase prayer to Him: "Be occupied with the one thing necessary, and let yourselves be guided by the Holy Spirit. Then your work will go well."[35] And also: "Abandon yourselves totally. I will protect you—I will pray to the Holy Spirit. Pray to Him yourselves."[36]

It is this renewed sense of the vital presence of the Holy Spirit in the lives of the faithful, as the soul of the universal Church in general, that is being requested by Mary in the message content.

3. Mary—Universal Mother and Intercessor

The specific role of Mary in the Medjugorjian event was made known on the third day of the apparitions (June 26, 1981), when she said: "I am the Blessed Virgin Mary. . . . I came here because there are many good believers here. I want to be with you, and to convert and reconcile all people."[37]

This message reflects the purpose of Mary in these apparitions: to convert and reconcile all people, to act as intercessor for humanity in a turning of heart away from sin and towards her Son. Her intercessory role is evident in her call to direct all prayers to Christ: "Please pray to Jesus. I am His Mother and I intercede for you to Him. But all prayers go to Jesus."[38] This is also the reference to Mary's role as a secondary mediator (or "mediatrix") of graces merited by Christ in the Thursday message to the parish received on May 17, 1984: "My Son Jesus wishes to bestow on you special graces through me."[39] Her universal intercession for humanity also comprises prayers and atonement to her Son for the countless sins which offend Him, as was her prayer on the Feast of the Immaculate Conception in 1981: "My beloved Son. Please forgive these numerous sins with which humanity is offending you."[40]

Beyond the role of intercessor, Mary has been presented in the message content as a loving Mother of humanity who seeks to bring to herself all people of the world as her children. This theme of endearing maternity surfaces in the following message on May 24, 1984: "Dear children! . . . I, your Mother, love you all. And in any moment when it is difficult for you, don't be afraid. I love you even when you are far from me and my Son."[41] And again in this Thursday message on November 29, 1984:

> Dear children! . . . Be aware, my beloved ones, that I am your Mother, and that I am coming upon the earth to teach you to listen out of love, to pray out of love, and to carry your cross, but not by force.[42]

The desire of Mary to have all of humanity feel her maternal love as her children is summarized in these two messages recently transmitted: "Dear children! I desire the whole world to become my children, but they are not willing. I want to give them everything. Pray, therefore."[43] And further: "Dear children! If you only knew how great my love is for you, you would cry with joy."[44]

4. Mass and Eucharistic Adoration

Since the message of Medjugorje is essentially Christological, then it follows without surprise that the content would also call for a strong devotion to Jesus Christ sacramentally but truly present in the Holy Eucharist. The gift of Christ to His faithful under the appearance of bread and wine is conveyed in this March 30, 1984 message encouraging daily Mass attendance:

> Children, I want the Holy Mass to be the gift of the day for you. Go to it; long for it to begin, because Jesus Christ Himself gives Himself to you during Mass. So, live for this moment when you are purified. Pray much that the Holy Spirit will renew your parish. If people assist at Mass in a half-hearted fashion, they will return with cold, empty hearts.[45]

The Mass, as the continuation of the sacrifice of Jesus Christ at Calvary, is denoted in this message as the greatest prayer given by God, the greatness of which cannot be comprehended.

> The Mass is the greatest prayer from God, and you will never understand the greatness of it. Therefore you must be perfect and humble at Mass, and you must prepare for it.[46]

Mary further invokes believers to participate in adoration of the Blessed Sacrament of the Altar, designated by her as a time of special graces:

> Adore continually the Most Holy Sacrament of the Altar. I am always present when the faithful are in adoration. Then special graces are being received.[47]

5. Sacramental Confession

The request for sacramental Confession appears early in the content of the message, with first mention occurring on June 26, 1981, the third day of the apparitions. Mary's call for reconciliation with God and with neighbor ends with the specific directive to receive the Sacrament of Reconciliation: "Men must be reconciled with God and with one another. For this to happen, it is necessary to believe, to pray, to fast, *and to go to Confession.*"[48] Mary has referred to the Sacrament of Reconciliation as a "medicine for the Church in the West", stating that "whole regions of the Church would be healed if believers would go to Confession once a month."[49]

The specification of Confession at least once a month was made at least as early as August 6, 1982, and was immediately implemented by the members of St. James parish.[50] But a later message transmitted by Jelena on November 7, 1983, admonishes against a type of mechanical Confession that is performed merely out of habit:

> Don't go to Confession from habit, only to stay the same after it. Confession should give force to your faith. It should stir you, and draw you near Jesus. If Confession does not mean much to you, you will be converted with great difficulty.[51]

6. The Rosary

The Rosary, that series of prayer and meditation upon the mysteries of the lives of Jesus and Mary, has been a principal form of prayer strongly requested in the messages.*

On the eve of the Feast of the Assumption, August 14, 1984, Ivan reported an unexpected apparition of Mary accompanied with this request for the full fifteen-decade Rosary every day: "I ask the people to pray with me these days. Pray all the more. . . . Say every day at least one Rosary: joyful, sorrowful, and glorious mysteries."[52]

Two later Thursday messages to the parish have reinforced the need of the Rosary as prayer for the fulfillment of Mary's plans for the parish and

---

* The parish youth group also prays what is called the "Rosary of Jesus Christ", a seven point meditation on the mysteries of Christ. The Rosary of Jesus appears in Appendix I.

for all people, and she specifically requests the Family Rosary to be said every night:

> Dear children! You have helped with your prayers for my plans to be fulfilled. Pray continually that they may be fulfilled to the full. I ask families of the parish to recite the Family Rosary.[53]

And in this Thursday message received by Jakov: "Dear children! Let all the prayers which you say in your houses in the evening be said for the conversion of sinners. . . . Pray the Rosary every evening."[54] The Rosary is unquestionably the fundamental form of devotional prayer requested in the Medjugorjian message.

7. Renewal of Sacred Scripture

A re-emphasis on the fruits of Sacred Scripture and its consistent use in daily prayer has been accentuated particularly in the messages transmitted through Jelena Vasilj. On April 19, 1984, the following message was reported by Jelena which reveals the spiritual strength obtained from a daily inplanting of the divine word into one's heart:

> I will tell you a spiritual secret: if you wish to be stronger than evil, make an active conscience for yourself. That is, pray a reasonable amount in the morning, read a text of Holy Scripture, and plant the divine word in your heart, and try to live it during the day, especially in moments of trial. So you will be stronger than evil.[55]

It was also through Jelena on March 1, 1984, that Mary requested the reading of the Scripture passage from the Gospel of Matthew (6:24-34) on every Thursday. Jelena has further reported the response of Mary on several occasions to the numerous questions posed to her as: "Why so many questions? The answer is in the Gospel."[56]

The emphasis on reading and praying Sacred Scripture is also present in this Thursday message to the parish:

> Dear children! Today I ask you to read the Bible in your houses every day and let it be in a visible place in the house, so that it will always encourage you to pray.[57]

8. Devotion to the Sacred Heart of Jesus and the Immaculate Heart of Mary

The devotion to the Hearts of Jesus and Mary, symbols of the divine and maternal love of Jesus and Mary for humanity, appears repeated times in the message content. One June 28, 1983, Jelena conveyed this message calling for a daily consecration of five minutes to the Sacred Heart: "Pray three hours a day. . . . You pray too little. . . . Consecrate five minutes to the Sacred Heart; every family is its image."[58]

Approximately one month later, Mary called for a consecration to her Immaculate Heart: "Consecrate yourselves totally to the Immaculate Heart. Abandon yourselves totally. I will protect you. . . ."[59] And this message of October 20, 1983, reiterates the need of a family consecration to the Sacred Heart of Jesus: "All families should consecrate themselves to the Sacred Heart every day."[60] Jelena has also received specific prayers of consecration both to the Sacred Heart of Jesus and the Immaculate Heart of Mary [see Appendix I].

It was during the Lenten season of 1984 that Mary requested a particular veneration of the Heart of her Son and His sacred wounds. This Thursday message towards the beginning of Lent called for the veneration of the sacred wounds of Christ, received because of human sin:

Dear children! This evening I am asking you in a special way during this Lent to honor the wounds of my Son, which He has received from the sins of this parish.[61]

And further, reparation and atonement to the Sacred Heart of Jesus for the unceasing sins of humanity is also the call in a Thursday message later in the same Lenten season:

This evening I am especially asking you to venerate the Heart of my Son, Jesus. Make an atonement for the wounds inflicted on the heart of my Son. That heart has been offended by all sorts of sins.[62]

Devotion, consecration, and the offering of reparation to the Hearts of Jesus and Mary, signs of their abundant love and mercy for humanity, are clearly grounded in the reported message content.

9. Heaven, Purgatory, Hell, and Satan

The reality of Heaven, Purgatory, Hell, and the active efforts of Satan in the world has been downplayed in contemporary society, but not in the content of the messages reported by the visionaries. The six visionaries have all reported to have seen Heaven, and those who did not ask to be spared the experience were also shown Purgatory and Hell.[63] During the experience of seeing Purgatory, Mary stated to the youths: "Those people are waiting for your prayers and sacrifices."[64]

In the interview with Mirjana, the visionary was asked by Fr. Tomislav Vlasic whether many people go to Hell today. Mirjana responded: "I asked her about that recently, and she said that today, most people go to Purgatory, the next greatest go to Hell, and only a few go directly to Heaven."[65]

In describing Purgatory, Mirjana reports different levels, and that most souls are released from Purgatory into Heaven on Christmas Day:

Then she told me that there are levels in Purgatory: levels closer to Hell and higher and higher toward Heaven. Most people, she said, think many souls are released from Purgatory into Heaven on All Saints' Day, but most souls are taken into Heaven on Christmas Day.[66]

The experience of Satan and his labors to counteract the plans of Mary in leading all people to the peace of Christ is a Medjugorjian theme repeated with intensity. The Thursday message to the parish received on August 11, 1984, points out the reality of Satan's efforts, and the need for a greater offering of self to Christ: "Satan is continually trying to thwart my plans. Pray with your heart, and in your prayer, give yourselves entirely to Jesus."[67] And two of the most recent Thursday messages of 1985 speak of the intensified works of Satan, and the disarming power of prayer: "In these days, Satan is fighting deviously against this parish. . . . Persevere in these days of temptation."[68] And further: ". . . Satan is working even more violently to take away the joy from each one of you. Through prayer, you can totally disarm him and ensure happiness."[69]

10. Ecumenism

The religious unity of Christians, of all peoples who worship the one God, and a sincere respect for other religions also presents itself in the content of the messages. The message reported by the visionaries which attests to the lack of religious division in the eyes of God, is careful to point out that while man has created religious division not intended by God, the one mediator to the Father remains Jesus Christ; and that one's particular religion is not a matter of indifference because the Holy Spirit is not equally present in every Church:

> In God's eyes, there are no divisions and there are no religions. You in the world have made the divisions. The one mediator is Jesus Christ. Which religion you belong to cannot be a matter of indifference. The presence of the Holy Spirit is not the same in every Church.[70]

Regarding the unnecessary segregation of members of different religions from each other, Mirjana conveys Mary's dislike of this separation:

> She also emphasized the failings of religious people, especially in small villages—for example, here in Medjugorje, where there is a separation from Serbians and Moslems. This separation is not good. The Madonna always stresses that there is but one God, and that people have enforced unnatural separation. One cannot truly believe, be a true Christian, if he does not respect other religions as well.[71]

Upon being questioned on the role of Jesus Christ if the Moslem religion is a good religion, Mirjana responded:

> We did not discuss that. She merely explained and deplored the lack of religious unity, "especially in the villages." She said that everybody's religion should be respected, and, of course, one's own.[72]

11. Family and Community Prayer

Family and community prayer, believers united in a single voice of praise to God, is presented in the Medjugorjian message content as a powerful means of combatting the plan of Satan to prevent the conversion of the world. It is particularly the need for families united in prayer that has been stressed, but there is also the strong invocation for community prayer.

Besides the call to daily Mass, where the Christian community led by the priest continues the sacrifice of Christ at Calvary, and celebrates a communal meal in the reception of His Body and Blood, Mary has also requested the formation of prayer groups in all parishes: "Yes, there is a need for a prayer group, not only in this parish, but in all parishes. Spiritual renewal is needed for the entire Church."[73]

Regarding the workings of Satan and his influence through the world, Mirjana reiterates the necessity posed by Mary for communal prayer, and in particular family prayer:

> The devil is not in them, but they're under the influence of the devil. To prevent this, at least to some extent, the Madonna said we need communal prayer, family prayer. She stressed the need for family prayer most of all.[74]

The recorded dialogue between Mary and Jelena illustrate the ability and the degree to which families can pray together:

> *Mary:*   I know that *every family* can pray four hours a day.
> *Jelena:*   But if I tell this to the people, they may back out.
> *Mary:*   Even you do not understand. It is only one sixth of the day.
> *Jelena:*   I know that you want us to pray continually.[75]

This recent Thursday message (November 1, 1984) reinforces the previous call to the Family Rosary in requesting a renewal of family prayer, and the retaining of its proper position in the hierarchy of priorities:

> Today I call you to the renewal of family prayer in your homes. The field work is over. Now all devote yourselves to prayer. Let family prayer take the first place in your families.[76]

12. Offering of Suffering and Sacrifice

On various occasions, Mary has requested or reinforced the spiritual practice of offering one's suffering and sacrifice to God—as a gift of the person's patient endurance of trials to God in reparation, and a willing acceptance of the events of Divine Providence. In a Thursday message transmitted during the 1984 Lenten season, Mary speaks of the people's reparational offering of their sacrifices in some type of participatory manner, as the incarnate God Himself endures His own continued sufferings: "Ponder how the Almighty is still suffering, because of your sins. So when the sufferings come, offer them as your sacrifice to God."[77]

A later Thursday message to the parish (October 4, 1984) contains a further reference to the offering of one's sufferings to Christ: ". . . Pray, therefore, that I may bring all your sufferings and prayers to the Lord."[78]

The theme of offering the sufferings endured in trial and testing continues in the Thursday message transmitted the following week, and requests a perpetual offering of burdens to God in faith and trust:

Thank you for your offering of all your pains to God, even now when He is testing you through the fruits which you are reaping [rain damage to a harvest crop]. Be aware, dear children, that He loves you, and for that reason He tests you. Always present your burdens to God and do not worry."[79]

13. Abandonment to God

The offering of daily trials in faith and trust leads into a complementary theme present in the content, namely the call of a total abandonment of self to God and His divine will. The nature of this self-abandonment to God does not constitute a quietistic withdrawal of all human effort in the day-to-day living of the Christian life. Abandonment comprises an unfailing trust and reliance on the workings of God in daily events of life as a perfection of Christian hope, and an active or passive response of loving obedience to the will of God, exemplified in the *fiat* of Mary at the Annunciation.

This June 16, 1983 message conveyed through Jelena calls for this total abandonment in a renouncing of disordered passions and a rejection of fear:

Abandon yourselves totally to God. Renounce disordered passions. Reject fear and give yourself; those who know how to abandon themselves will no longer know either fear or obstacles.[80]

The Gospel passage transmitted through Jelena to be read every Thursday (Matthew 6:24-34) is a profound call to a deeper trust and faith in the Heavenly Father who knows all our needs, to put aside anxieties of tomorrow, and to "seek first of all His kingdom and His righteousness and all these things shall be yours."[81]

In the further message through Jelena, Mary speaks of the continued efforts of Satan towards those who abandon themselves: "Those who give themselves to God will be the objects of attack."[82]

Finally, Mary renews the calls to abandonment to God, particularly in the light of Satan's juxtaposed labors: "Dear children! Pray, because Satan is continually trying to thwart my plans. Pray with your hearts and in prayer *give yourselves up to Jesus.*"[83]

14. Eschatological Urgency

A strand of urgency that calls for an immediate conversion of heart based on a pending forthcoming world chastisement can be traced throughout the message of Medjugorje. This is certainly evident in the report written by Fr. Vlasic and the visionaries sent to Rome in November, 1983. Here is an extract from that report which speaks of the brevity of time for conversion in the light of some significant upcoming world event:

> After the first admonition, the others will follow in a rather short time. Thus people will have some time for conversion. That interval will be a period of grace and conversion. After the visible sign appears, those who are still alive will have little time for conversion. For that reason, the Blessed Virgin invites us to urgent conversion and reconciliation.[84]

In the interview with Mirjana, the only visionary who claims to have received the tenth secret at present, one finds the same imperative to immediate conversion and spiritual preparation regarding the possibility of people to prepare for what is to come. Mirjana states:

> Yes, prepare! The Madonna said people should prepare themselves spiritually, be ready, and not panic; be reconciled in their souls. They should be ready for the worst, to die tomorrow. They should accept God now so that they will not be afraid. No one accepts death easily, but they can be at peace with their souls if they are believers.[85]

Also present in the content with regard to the theme of eschatalogical urgency are the references to the apparitions of Mary at Medjugorje as the last series of apparitions on earth, as seen here in the response of Mirjana to questions concerning this apparition:

Mirjana:	I asked her why, why I had to be the first [to cease receiving the apparitions]. She said that she stayed with us for a long time, longer than is necessary, but that this is the last apparition on earth. . . .
Fr. Vlasic:	What do you mean, "the last apparition on earth"?
Mirjana:	It is the last time Jesus or Mary will appear on earth.
Fr. Vlasic:	What do you mean, "appear"?
Mirjana:	The last time they will appear as they have, so that you can speak with them.
Fr. Vlasic:	You mean that this is the last apparition in this era, in this period of the Church, or that they will never again come to earth?

Mirjana: I don't know. The Madonna said this is the last apparition on earth.[86]

The consistent focus of the call to convert possesses an unmistakable
urgency, as is conveyed in this Spring, 1983 dispatch:

> Hasten your conversion. *Do not wait* for the sign that has been announced
> for the unbelievers; it will already be too late for them to have a conversion.
> You who believe, be converted and deepen your faith.[87]

Summary Statement

The synthesis of the subject matter of the message reported by the
visionaries at Medjugorje into thematic and doctrinal categories again is
not a comprehensive content, nor doctrinal summary of everything
contained in the individual messages. The division of the content into the
six foundational themes (faith, prayer, fasting, penance, conversion, and
peace), and the fourteen developmental themes (Jesus Christ—the One
Redeemer and Mediator; Renewal in the Holy Spirit; Mary—Universal
Mother and Intercessor; Mass and Eucharastic Adoration; Sacramental
Confession; The Rosary; Renewal of Sacred Scripture; Devotion to the
Sacred Heart of Jesus and the Immaculate Heart of Mary; Heaven,
Purgatory, Hell, and Satan; Ecumenism; Family and Community Prayer;
Offering of Suffering and Sacrifices; Abandonment to God; and Escha-
talogical Urgency) is an effort to locate the vast majority of the doctrine
and content into logical categories that serve to summarize the major
emphases of the message of Medjugorje.

Let us proceed to an examination of the presence of the six foundational
themes of the message of Medjugorje as they are found in the Gospels of
the New Testament and the writings of the Apostolic Fathers.

Notes
Chapter Two

[1] René Laurentin, *Is the Virgin Appearing?*, Washington, The Word Among Us Press, 1984, p. 88.

2 Cf. *supra*, Chapter I, section 1. Note: All quoted messages will be taken from the various sections of Chapter I of this work and will be noted accordingly.

[3] Cf. *supra*, Chapter I, section 4.

[4] Cf. *supra*, Chapter I, section 3.

[5] Cf. *supra*, Chapter I, section 1.

[6] Cf. *supra*, Chapter I, section 6.

[7] *Ibid.*

[8] Cf. *supra*, Chapter I, section 6.

[9] *Ibid.*

[10] Cf. *supra*, Chapter I, section 2.

[11] Cf. *supra*, Chapter I, section 7. Note: Up to this time, the parish had only been asked to fast strictly on Fridays.

[12] Cf. *supra*, Chapter I, section 2.

[13] Cf. *supra*, Chapter I, section 7.

[14] Cf. *supra*, Chapter I, section 2.

[15] Cf. *supra*, Chapter I, section 7.

[16] Cf. *supra*, Chapter I, section 4.

[17] Cf. *supra*, Chapter I, section 5.

[18] Cf. *supra*, Chapter I, section 2.

[19] Cf. *supra*, Chapter I, section 4.

[20] Cf. *supra*, Chapter I, section 2.

[21] Cf. *supra*, Chapter I, section 7.

[22] *Ibid.*

[23] Cf. *supra*, Chapter I, section 1.

[24] Cf. *supra*, Chapter I, section 4.

[25] Cf. *supra*, Chapter I, section 6.

[26] Cf. *supra*, Chapter I, section 7.

[27] Cf. *supra*, Chapter I, section 1.

[28] Cf. *supra*, Chapter I, section 2.

[29] Cf. *supra*, Chapter I, section 3.

[30] *Ibid.*

[31] *Ibid.*

[32] Cf. *supra*, Chapter I, section 6.

[33] Cf. *supra*, Chapter I, section 7.

[34] *Ibid.*

[35] Cf. *supra*, Chapter I, section 6.

[36] *Ibid.*

[37] Cf. *supra*, Chapter I, section 1.

[38] Cf. *supra*, Chapter I, section 3.
[39] Cf. *supra*, Chapter I, section 7.
[40] Cf. *supra*, Chapter I, section 2.
[41] Cf. *supra*, Chapter I, section 7.
[42] *Ibid.*
[43] Cf. *supra*, Chapter I, section 8.
[44] *Ibid.*
[45] Cf. *supra*, Chapter I, section 6.
[46] Cf. *supra*, Chapter I, section 3.
[47] Cf. *supra*, Chapter I, section 7.
[48] Cf. *supra*, Chapter I, section 1.
[49] Cf. *supra*, Chapter I, section 3.
[50] Cf. *supra*, Chapter I, section 3.
[51] Cf. *supra*, Chapter I, section 6.
[52] Cf. *supra*, Chapter I, section 7.
[53] *Ibid.*
[54] *Ibid.*
[55] Cf. *supra*, Chapter I, section 6.
[56] *Ibid.*
[57] Cf. *supra*, Chapter I, section 7.
[58] Cf. *supra*, Chapter I, section 6.
[59] *Ibid.*
[60] *Ibid.*
[61] Cf. *supra*, Chapter I, section 7.
[62] *Ibid.*
[63] Cf. *supra*, Chapter I, section 3.
[64] *Ibid.*
[65] Cf. *supra*, Chapter I, section 4.
[66] *Ibid.*
[67] Cf. *supra*, Chapter I, section 7.
[68] *Ibid.*
[69] *Ibid.*
[70] Cf. *supra*, Chapter I, section 3.
[71] Cf. *supra*, Chapter I, section 4.
[72] *Ibid.*
[73] Cf. *supra*, Chapter I, section 3.
[74] Cf. *supra*, Chapter I, section 4.
[75] Cf. *supra*, Chapter I, section 6.
[76] Cf. *supra*, Chapter I, section 7.
[77] *Ibid.*
[78] *Ibid.*
[79] *Ibid.*
[80] Cf. *supra*, Chapter I, section 6.
[81] *Ibid.*
[82] *Ibid.*
[83] Cf. *supra*, Chapter I, section 7.
[84] Cf. *supra*, Chapter I, section 5.
[85] Cf. *supra*, Chapter I, section 4.
[86] *Ibid.*
[87] Cf. *supra*, Chapter I, section 2.

CHAPTER THREE

Presence of the Medjugorje Foundational Content in the Gospels and the Apostolic Fathers

The six foundational themes that arise from the content of the message of Medjugorje are the following: faith, prayer, fasting, penance, conversion, and peace. Let us examine the presence of the same six themes in the Gospels of the New Testament, the revealed Word of Jesus Christ, and the writings of the Apostlic Fathers, the earliest non-canonical writings of the early Christian community.*

Faith

1. Faith in the Gospels

The call to "believe" by Jesus Christ is an essential call manifested in his "Good News" of salvation, as is also found present in the Medjugorjian message. In the Gospel of Mark, the call to faith comprises the first words to come from the lips of Christ:. "Now after John was arrested, Jesus came into Galilee, preaching the gospel of God, and saying 'the time is fulfilled, and the kingdom of God is at hand; repent and believe in the Gospel.' " (Mark 1:14-15).[1]

In the Gospel of John, Jesus poses the responses of faith as that effort which constitutes the work of God: "Then they [the crowd] said to Him, 'What must we do to be doing the work of God?' Jesus answered them, 'This is the work of God, that you believe in Him whom He has sent.' " (John 6:28-29).

And to the apostles during the Last Supper, Jesus calls for faith, both in Him and in the Father: "Let your hearts not be troubled: believe in God, believe also in Me." (John 14:1).

A living faith is also accentuated in the Gospels, as is also the case in

---

* This does not propose to be either a comprehensive scriptural or patrological treatment the six themes in question, but an illustration of the clear presence of the themes in the Gospels and the Apostolic Fathers.

the message of Medjugorje, as the gateway both to the miraculous on earth and the glories and salvation of eternal life in heaven. St. John speaks of the effects of a living faith in the following passage:

> For God so loved the world that He gave His only Son, that whoever believes in Him should not perish but have eternal life. For God sent the Son into the world, not to condemn the world, but that the world might be saved through Him. (John 3:16-17).

And further from the Gospel according to John: "For this is the will of My Father, that everyone who sees the Son and believes in Him should have eternal life; and I will raise him up on the last day" (John 6:40). And further: "Truly, truly, I say to you, he who hears my words and believes Him who sent me, has eternal life; he does not come into judgement, but has passed from death to life." (John 5:24).

As to the powerful effect of a living faith in this world, the Gospel of Matthew speaks of the possibility of the miraculous for those who believe (visible at the occasion of the withering of the fig tree):

> When the disciples saw it, they marvelled, saying, "How did the fig tree wither at once?" And Jesus answered them, "Truly I say to you, if you have faith and never doubt, you will not only do what has been done to the fig tree, but even if you say to this mountain, 'Be taken up and cast into the sea,' it will be done. And whatever you ask in prayer, you will receive, if you have faith." (Matt. 21:19-22).

Christ has not hesitated to state in the Gospels that firm faith can be an impetus for the miraculous. This is evident in the passage of the woman with the hemorrhage, where the faith of the woman was the necessary pre-condition of her cure:

> And behold, a woman who had suffered from a hemorrhage for twelve years came up behind him and touched the fringe of his garment; for she said to herself, "If I only touch his garment, I shall be made well." Jesus turned and seeing her he said, "Take heart, my daughter, your faith has made you well." And instantly, the woman was made well. (Matt. 9:20-22).

The same essential pre-condition of faith is evident in the curing of the two blind men:

> And as Jesus passed on from there, two blind men followed him, crying aloud, "Have mercy on us, Son of David." When he entered the house, the blind men came to him; and Jesus said to them, "Do you believe that I am able to do this?" They said to him, "Yes Lord". Then he touched their eyes, saying, "according to your faith be it done to you." And their eyes were opened. (Matt. 9:27-30).

But ultimately, the call to faith comes down to the crucial eschatalogical question asked by Christ Himself: "Nevertheless, when the Son of Man comes, will he find faith on earth?" (Luke 18:8).

The imperative to "believe" is unquestionably a life-saving call in the words of Jesus Christ, which finds its parallel in the message of Medjugorje.

2. *Faith in the Apostolic Fathers*

The call to faith in the Apostlic Fathers is first evident in the *Letter to the Corinthians* written by St. Clement of Rome (c. 92-101 A.D.), third papal successor to St. Peter. St. Clement exhorts the Christian community at Corinth to fix faithfully their minds on God so as to be among the recipients of the blessed gifts of God: "Let us strive, therefore, to be found in the number of those who wait for Him, that we may share in the promised gifts. But how shall this be, beloved? If our minds be fixed by *means of faith on God*." (1 Cor. 35:4-5).[2]

In the *Letter to the Ephesians*, St. Ignatius of Antioch (c. 97-118 A.D.) speaks of the power of a unified faith against the forces of Satan in a manner quite similar to that seen in the message of Medjugorje: "Make an effort, then, to meet more frequently to celebrate God's Eucharist and to offer praise. For, when you meet frequently in the same place, the forces of Satan are overthrown, and his baneful influence is neutralized by the *unanimity of your faith*." (Eph. 13:1-2).[3]

The early bishop of Antioch further calls for a perfect faith joined by perfect love: "You are aware of all these truths if you have perfect faith and love for Jesus Christ—the beginning and end of life; for faith is the beginning and the end is love and God is the two of them brought into unity." (Eph. 14:1).[4]

The *Didache* (the Teaching of the Twelve Apostles, c. 60-120 A.D.) calls both for a lifelong faith leading to perfection, and a perseverence of faith through the period of final testing: "Come together frequently, and seek what pertains to your souls; for the whole time of your faith will not profit you, unless in the last hour you shall be found perfect. . . . When shall all created men come to the fire of judgement, and 'many will be scandalized' and perish; but those who persevere in faith will be saved from the curse itself." (Did. 16:2, 5).[5]

Lastly, in the *Letter to the Phillipians*, St. Polycarp, bishop of Smyrna (c. 135 A.D.) calls the community to a growth in their faith and truth: "May the God and Father of Our Lord Jesus Christ, and the Eternal High Priest Himself, the Son of God, Jesus Christ, further your growth in faith and truth, and in meekness that is perfect. . . ." (Phil. 12:2)[6]

Faith as found in the Gospels and the Apostolic Fathers points to the same nature of faith visible in the message of Medjugorje: a belief in Christ that offers heavenly salvation, and the earthly condition for the miraculous; or an unbelief that leads to "scandal at the fire of judgement."[7]

Prayer

1. Prayer in the Gospels

The insistent call to prayer present in the message of Medjugorje is oftentimes emphasized by the emphatic phrase: "Pray! Pray! Pray!" The same imperative to pray and an attestation to its powerful effects resound in the Good News of Jesus Christ.

Christ transmits the call to pray principally through His own example of prayer. After a series of miracles and healings the previous day, Christ begins the morning in solitary prayer: "And he healed many who were sick with various diseases, and cast out many demons. . . . And in the morning, a great while before day, he rose and went out to a lonely place, and there he prayed." (Mk. 1:34-35).

And another example of solitary prayer that provides the spiritual foundation for this public ministry appears in the Gospel according to St. Matthew: "And after he had dismissed the crowds, he went up into the hills by himself to pray. When evening came he was still there alone. . . ." (Matt. 14:23).

And in the Gospel of John, Jesus makes known His own prayer for those who believe in Him, for their protection against Satan, and for their unity in Christ and the Father:

> I am not praying for the world, but for those whom thou has given me, for they are thine, and I am glorified in them. . . . I do not pray that thou shouldst take them out of the world, but that thou shouldst keep them from the evil one. . . . I do not pray for these only, but also for those who believe in Me through their word, that they may all be one; even as Thou, Father, art in Me, and I in Thee. . . . (John 17:9-10, 15, 20-21).

Christ illustrates the imperative to pray, particularly in the midst of trial, as He Himself prepared for the Passion to come by prayer at the Mount of Olives:

> And he withdrew from them (the disciples) about a stone's throw, and knelt down and prayed, "Father, if thou art willing, remove this cup from me; nevertheless, not my will, but thine be done." And there appeared to him an angel strengthening him. And being in agony, he prayed more earnestly; and his sweat became like great drops of blood falling down upon the ground. And when he rose from prayer, he came to his disciples. . . . (Lk. 22:41-45).

Jesus further calls his followers to pray, instructs them how to pray, and tells them for what they should be praying, all of which is summarized in the prayer Christ gives:

> And when you pray, you must not be like the hypocrites; for they love to stand in prayer in the synagogues and at the street corners, that they may be

seen by men. Truly, I say to you, they have their reward. But when you pray, go into your room and shut the door and pray to Your Father who is in secret; and Your Father who is in secret will reward you. And in praying do not heap up empty phrases, as the Gentiles do, for they think that they will be heard for their many words. Do not be like them, for Your Father knows what you need before you ask him. Pray then like this:

Our Father who art in Heaven,
Hallowed by thy Name.
Thy kingdom come,
Thy will be done,
On earth as it is in heaven.
Give us this day our daily bread;
And forgive us our debts,
As we also have forgiven our debtors;
And lead us not into temptation
But deliver us from evil. (Matt. 6:7-13).

The profound effects of prayer also ring clear in the words of Christ: "Therefore I tell you, whatever you ask in prayer, believe that you receive it, and you will." (Mk. 11:24-25).

2. Prayer in the Apostolic Fathers

The call to prayer is also a strong mandate in the writings of the Apostolic Fathers, and is first found in the *Didache*. Amidst opening exhortations to "pray for your enemies" and "pray for others", the teaching of the Twelve Apostles specifies praying the Lord's Prayer three times daily:

And do not pray as the hypocrites do, but pray as the Lord has commanded in the gospel, pray thus: "Our Father, who art in heaven. . . ." Pray thus three times a day. (Did. 8:1-3).[8]

St. Ignatius of Antioch makes repeated references to the irreplaceable position of prayer in the Christian life. In his *Letter to Polycarp*, Ignatius calls for unceasing prayer, greatly resembling Mary's request for continual prayer: "To prayer give yourself unceasingly; being for an increase in understanding; watch without letting your spirit flag." (Poly. 1:3).[9]

And in his *Letter to the Ephesians* Ignatius calls for constant prayer for conversions, also in echo of the Medjugorjian call: "But pray *unceasingly* also for the rest of men, for they offer ground for hoping that they may be converted and win their way to God." (Eph. 10:1).[10]

The call to pray unceasingly, to pray in the midst of trial, to pray for conversions, to community prayer, and the ability of prayer in disarming the efforts of Satan all comprise principal points of convergence with the Medjugorjian request to "Pray, pray, pray".

Fasting

1. Fasting in the Gospels

The message of Medjugorje presents a call to fasting, and in its latest form (August 14, 1984) Mary called the parish of St. James to fast strictly (on bread and water) every Wednesday and Friday. The presence of fasting is likewise found in the Gospels, again beginning with the example of Christ Himself.

Immediately following his baptism in the Jordan by John, Jesus consented to the call of the Holy Spirit to enter the wilderness to be tempted by Satan. But the manner in which Christ chose to prepare Himself for this period of temptations was precisely the discipline of fasting:

> Then Jesus was led up by the Spirit into the wilderness to be tempted by the devil. And he fasted forty days and forty nights, and afterwards was hungry. And the temptor came and said to him, "If you are the Son of God, summon these stones to become loaves of bread". But he answered, "It is written, 'Man shall not live by bread alone, but every word that proceeds from the mouth of God.'" (Matt. 4:1-5).

When Christ presents His teaching in regard to fasting, He simply presumes that those He is instructing are in fact performing the discipline:

> And when you fast, do not look dismal, like the hypocrites, for they disfigure their faces that their fasting may be seen by men. Truly, I say to you, they have their reward. But when you fast, anoint your head and wash your face, that your fasting may not be seen by men but by Your heavenly Father who is in secret; and Your Father who sees you in secret will reward you. (Matt. 6:6-18).

When the disciples of John question Jesus as to why his disciples do not fast like they and the Pharisees, He makes it clear that upon the departure of the bridegroom, the disciples of Christ also will fast:

> Then the disciples of John came to him saying, "Why do we and the Pharisees fast, but your disciples do not fast?" And Jesus said to them, "Can the wedding guests mourn as long as the bridegroom is with them? The days will come when the bridegroom is taken away from them, and then they will fast." (Matt. 9:14-16).

Christ further accentuates the power of the discipline of fasting, in particular when it is united with fervent prayer, in this example of the possessed boy whom the disciples of Jesus tried to cure but could not. The passage highlights the spiritual force of faith, prayer, and fasting against the presence of evil, comprising a recognizable parallel to the Medjugorjian message:

The disciples approached Jesus at that point and asked him privately, "Why could we not expel it?" "Because you have so little trust," he told them. "I assure you, if you had faith the size of a mustard seed, you would be able to say to this mountain, 'Move from here to there,' and it would move. This kind does not leave but by *prayer and fasting*." (Matt. 17:19-21).[11]

2. Fasting in the Apostolic Fathers

A firm indication of the existence of fasting in the early Christian community is located in the Teaching of the Twelve Apostles (Didache). An unquestionable similarity with the message of Medjugorje appears in the directive on fasting found in the eighth chapter (almost as if Mary at Medjugorje were calling for a return to early Church ascetical practices): "But do not let your fasts be with the hypocrites, for they fast on Mondays and Thursdays; but you shall fast on Wednesday and Friday." (Did. 8:1).[12]

There is also the instruction to the early Christian community to fast for the benefit of others (in particular for one's persecutors): "Bless those who curse you, and pray for your enemies, *and fast* for those that persecute you." (Did. 1:2).[13]

Further, both those preparing to receive the sacrament of baptism and entry into the Church (and those who are to administer the sacrament) are called to fast: "But before the baptism, let the one who baptizes and the one to be baptized fast, and any others who are able to do so. And you shall require the person being baptised to fast for one or two days." (Did. 7:4).[14]

Both the obligation of Christian fasting and its specification of being done on Wednesdays and Fridays, present in the message of Medjugorje, is likewise evident in the practice of fasting visible in the Gospels and the writings from the infant Church.

Penance

1. Penance in the Gospels

The call to penance in the Message of Medjugorje comprises that general category of physical and spiritual self-denial which is performed for the sake of Christ (of which fasting is a major constituent). Because the general category of penance could be extended in the Gospels to such an all-encompassing degree (for example, from the evangelical counsels, to fasting, to the crucifixion of Christ), we will refer to the presence of penance in the Gospels according to the words of Christ that establish the principal for all forms of physical self-denial for the sake of man's spiritual dimension.

In the Gospel of Matthew, Jesus establishes the justification of the denial and mortification of the body for the good of the soul:

> If your right eye causes you sin, pluck it out and throw it away; it is better that you lose one of your members than that your whole body be thrown into hell. And if your right hand causes you to sin, cut it off and throw it away; it is better that you lose one of your members than that your whole body go into hell. (Matt. 5:27-30).

Here one sees the call to subordinate the desires of the body to the good of the spirit, and to perform acts of physical mortification so as to safeguard the life of the soul. It is these words of Christ that call all Christians to incorporate the discipline of penance into their lives, which is exemplified but not exhausted in the physical self-denial of fasting.

2. Penance in the Apostolic Fathers

The only specific mention of the general concept of penance in the Apostlic Fathers[15] appears in the *Letter to the Corinthians* by St. Clement of Rome. St. Clement offers the praiseworthy example of Queen Esther, who for the spiritual welfare of her people, chastised her body so as to offer these sufferings as intercession to the God of the Ages:

> Nor did Esther, that woman of perfect faith, expose herself to less danger in order to rescue the twelve tribes of Israel from imminent destruction; for by fasting and chastising her body she implored the All-Seeing Master, the God of the Ages, and He, seeing her self-abasement, rescued the people for whose sake she had incurred danger." (1 Cor. 55:6).[16]

Conversion

1. Conversion in the Gospels

Conversion is a crucial element in the message of Medjugorje, and it comprises the pre-requisite that enables an affirmative response to the other various demands for which Mary has petitioned. The call to conversion, a turning of heart away from sin and egocentrism and towards God and Christocentrism, resounds also in the Gospels.*

The call to conversion appears first in the Gospels from the lips of John the Baptist, upon whose feast day, June 24, marks the first reported Marian apparition at Medjugorje. With a pointed unambiguity, he

---

* The call to conversion is also exceptionally strong in the Acts of the Apostles, particularly to be found in the Post-Pentecostal speeches of Peter and Paul.

preaches the need for a baptism of repentance in preparation for the one who is to come:

> In those days came *John the Baptist*, preaching in the wilderness of Judea. "Repent, for the kingdom of heaven is at hand." For this is he who was spoken of by the prophet Isaiah when he said, "The voice of one crying in the wilderness. Prepare the way of the Lord, make his path straight." (Matt. 3:1-3).

Yet upon the arrival of the multitudes for this baptism of repentance (including both Pharisees and Sadduccees), John demands to see some external sign of their conversion of heart, the fruits befitting an authentic repentance:

> He said therefore to the multitudes that came out to be baptised by him, "You brood of vipers, who warned you to flee from the wrath to come? Bear fruit that befits repentance', and do not begin to say to yourselves, 'We have Abraham as our Father'; for I tell you, God is able from these stones to raise up children to Abraham. Even now the axe is laid to the root of the tree. Every tree, therefore, that does not bear good fruit is cut down and thrown into the fire." (Lk. 3:7-9)

Christ Himself makes His universal call to conversion evident in answering the charges of the Pharisees for dining with the tax collectors and sinners:

> And the Pharisees and their scribes murmured against his disciples, saying, "Why do you eat and drink with tax collectors and sinners?" And Jesus answered them, "Those who are well have no need for a physician, but those who are sick; I have not come to call the righteous, but sinners to repentance." (Lk 5:30-32).

In the Gospel according to St. Luke, Jesus describes the heavenly joy over the conversion of a single sinner in the parable of the lost sheep:

> What man of you, having a hundred sheep, if he has lost one of them, does not leave the ninety-nine in the wilderness, and go after the one which is lost until he finds it? And when he has found it, he lays it on his shoulders, rejoicing. And when he comes home, he calls together his friends and his neighbors, saying to hem, "Rejoice with me, for I have found my sheep which is lost." Just so I tell you, there will be more joy in heaven over one sinner who repents than over ninety-nine righteous persons who need no repentence. (Lk. 15:4-8).

The essential element for true conversion as it appears repeatedly in the Gospels is repentance. It is repentance that allows for the forgiveness of sins (Mk. 1:4), which enables a flowering of conversion into a living faith (Mk. 1:15). But for anyone who fails to consistently repent, to ask repeatedly for forgiveness of their sins in a continual turning of their hearts from self to God, Jesus does not hesitate to make known the effects of this hardness of heart.

Upon being informed of those Galileans "whose blood Pilate had mingled with their sacrifices", Jesus is quick to eliminate the idea that the present age is in any less need to conversion than those Galileans in question: "Do you think that these Galileans were worse sinners than all the other Galileans, because they suffered thus? I tell you, no; but unless you repent you will likewise perish." (Lk. 13:2-4).

In the same manner, Christ remonstrates anyone (and in this case those in the temple) who would think conversion a good thing only for the "prostitutes" and "tax collectors" but not for themselves:

> Truly, I say to you, the tax collectors and the harlots go into the kingdom of God before you. For John came to you in the way of righteousness, and you did not believe him, but the tax collectors and harlots believed him, and even when you saw it, you did not afterward repent and believe him. (Matt. 21:31-32).

Finally, in the Gospel of John, reference is made to the fulfillment of the prophecy of Isaiah in describing those who refuse to turn and believe, even after a numerous display of signs and miracles:

> Though he [Jesus] had done so many signs before them, yet they did not believe in him; it was that the word spoken by the prophet Isaiah might be fulfilled. . . . "He has blinded their eyes and hardened their hearts, lest they should see with their eyes and perceive with their heart, and turn to Me to heal them." (Jn. 12:37, 39-40).

2. Conversion to the Apostolic Fathers

The call to conversion in the Apostolic Fathers begins with the moving passage from St. Clement's *Letter to the Corinthians*. Here the third papal successor of St. Peter cites these moving Old Testament calls to conversion, echoing the Medjugorjian call to convert:

> The minister of the grace of God exhorted through the Holy Spirit to conversion, and the Master of the Universe Himself exhorted to conversion with an oath: "As I truly live, says the Lord, I do not desire the death of the sinner, but his conversion. . . . House of Israel, be converted from your iniquity. . . . Should your sins reach from earth to heaven, and should they be redder than scarlet and blacker than sack-cloth, and should you turn to me with all your heart and say, 'Father!', I will listen to you as a consecrated People." And in another passage He says as follows: "Wash and be cleansed and put away from your souls the wickedness which offends my eyes, rid yourselves of your evil doings, learn to do good, strive for justice, rescue the oppressed, sustain the rights of the orphan, and see justice be done to the widows. . . . And should your sins be like purple, I will make them white as snow; and should they be like scarlet, I will make them white as wool; and if you are willing and listen to me, you shall eat the good things of the land; but if you are not willing and do not listen to me, the sword shall devour you. Thus the mouth of the Lord has spoken." It follows that He wants all His beloved to have a chance to be converted, and this He has ratified by His Almighty will.
> Therefore, let us comply with His Magnificent and Glorious purpose,

and let us crave His Mercy and loving-kindness on bended knee, and burn to His compassion, after abandoning our vain efforts and our strife and jealousy which but leads to death. (1 Cor. 8, 9:1).[17]

St. Clement also accentuates the role of Christ in the grace of conversion, and how it is a call to all generations:

Let us fix our eyes upon the Blood of Christ and understand how precious it is to the Father, because, poured out for our salvation, it brought the whole world the grace of conversion. Let us pass in review of all generations and learn the lesson, that from generation to generation, the Master has given an opportunity for conversion to those who were willing to turn to Him (1 Cor. 7:4-5).[18]

And in the oldest Eucharistic prayer of thanksgiving found in the *Didache*, the primitive canon ends with a final petition both for the converted and the unconverted:

Hosanna to the God of David
If anyone is holy, let him advance:
If anyone is not, let him be converted!
Marana tha![19]

Finally, in the *Letter to the Ephesians*, St. Ignatius of Antioch calls for an unceasing prayer for the conversion of all humanity: "But pray unceasingly also for the rest of men, for they offer ground for hoping that they may be converted and win their way to God." (Eph. 10:1).[20]

The call to conversion, achieved through a resolute and continual repentance, resounds both in the words of Christ, John the Baptist, and St. Clement of Rome, and in the content of the message of Medjugorje. All these sources unquestionably exclaim the need to "hasten your conversion"[21] or "likewise perish".[22]

Peace

1. Peace in the Gospels

From the commencement of the reported apparitions, the call to peace has been central in the contents of the message of Medjugorje, and appears to be a goal upon which all the other directives converge; for it is a peace of heart that is obtained only through faith, prayer, fasting, penance, and conversion. The gift of peace offered by Christ, and the references to peace as a fundamental goal in the Christian life can also be found in the Gospels.

In the Gospel of John, Christ describes His gift of peace as tranquility of heart, the nature of which this world is incapable of providing: "Peace

I leave with you; my peace I give to you; not as the world gives do I give it to you. Let not your hearts be troubled, neither let them be afraid.'' (Jn. 14:27).

It is also significant that upon the first two occasions when the risen Christ appeared to the disciples as recorded in John's Gospel, the first words spoken by Christ pertain to His gift of peace:

> On the evening of that day, the first day of the week, the doors being shut where the disciples were, for fear of the Jews, Jesus came and stood among them and said to them, "Peace be with you." When He had said this, He showed them His hands and His side. Then His disciples were glad that they saw the Lord. Jesus said to them again, "Peace be with you." (Jn. 20:19-20). . . .
>
> "Eight days later, His disciples were again in the house, and Thomas was with them. The doors were shut, but Jesus came and stood among them, and said, "Peace be with you!" (Jn. 20:26).

During His public ministry, Christ granted His gift of peace to individuals, which oftentimes followed a manifestation of His identity through miracles and healings (almost as a gift apart from the gift of healing that likewise comes as a result of their faith). This is evident in the healing of the woman with a hemorrhage: "Daughter, your faith has made you well, go in peace, and be healed of your disease" (Mk. 5:34); and in the pardon of Christ to the penitent woman who anointed Him: "And he said to the woman, 'Your faith has saved you; go in peace.' '' (Lk. 7:50).

The gift of peace seems to have accompanied Christ and entered the world from the very moment of His birth, as proclaimed by the multitude of angels in their Christmas praise: "Glory to God in the highest, and on earth peace among men with whom he is pleased." (Lk. 2:17).

Part of the mission of Christ's disciples was to bring the gift of peace to those with open hearts: "Whatever house you enter, first say, 'Peace be to this house!' And if a son of peace is there, your peace shall rest upon him; but if not, it shall return to you." (Lk. 10:5-6).

But this gift of interior peace should not be left dormant and individual, but should also flower into a peace of family, of community, and of society. The beatitudes praise the peacemakers, who should partake in the spreading of a social peace firmly founded on the interior peace of Christ (Matt. 5:9); and this message from Christ found in Mark reaffirms the need for the ''salt of the earth'' to remain in peace amidst themselves: "Salt is good, but if the salt has lost its saltiness, how will you season it? Have salt in yourselves and *be at peace with one another.*" (Mk. 9:50).

Peace is further offered in the Gospel as a goal of the Christian life, and a foreshadowing taste of the ultimate peace to be experienced in the glory of eternal life. The words of Simeon upon recognizing the Christ child as the promised Messiah illustrate the desire to "depart in peace":

Lord, now lettest thou thy servant
depart in peace,
according to your work;
for mine eyes have seen the salvation
which thou has preparest in the
presence of all peoples,
a light for revelation to the Gentiles,
and for glory to thy people Israel. (Lk. 2:29-32).

The Canticle of Zechariah also points to peace as the path for those who are to follow the Lord, who will: ". . . give light to those who sit in darkness and the shadow of death, to guide our feet into the way of peace." (Lk. 1:79).

Yet the Gospels again speak to the reality that not all will accept the gift of Christ's peace. As Christ nears the city of Jerusalem, He weeps out of sorrow for those refusing to accept His message, His gift, and His life of peace, the result of which will eventually lead to the destruction of Jerusalem. In His sorrow, Jesus speaks words that call our own generation to reflect upon: "Would that even today you know the things that make for peace!" (Lk. 19:41).

But even in the midst of the peacelessness of the world, Christ reassures those who believe in Him of His final victory over earthly tribulation, through the peace *found only in Him*: "I have said this to you, that in Me you may have peace. In the world, you have tribulation, but be of good cheer, I have overcome the world." (Jn. 16:33).

2. Peace in the Apostolic Fathers

The theme of peace in the Apostlic Fathers can be cited in St. Clement of Rome's Letter to the Corinthians. The bishop of Rome and head of the early Church cites peace as the goal of the life of the faith handed down from the days of the patriarchs:

And so, since we are allowed to profit by so many glorious examples, let us hasten on the goal of peace handed down to us from the beginning, and let us fix our gaze upon the Father and Creator of the whole world and hold fast to the magnificent and superabundant gifts and blessings of peace. (1 Cor. 19:2).[23]

St. Clement quotes the Psalms in the foreshadowing of Christ and His precepts in again establishing peace as one of those precepts: "To all these precepts the faith in Christ gives stability; for He Himself through the Holy Spirit calls us to Him as follows: . . . seek peace and go in pursuit of it." (1 Cor. 22:5).[24]

And further, in this prayer for peace in its social dimension: "Yes, Master, let Thy face beam upon us, that we may do good in peace. . . . Grant concord and peace to us and all the other inhabitants of the earth. . . ." (1 Cor. 60:3).[25]

St. Ignatius of Antioch, in his *Letter to the Ephesians*, gives a profound summary of both spiritual and social peace, and its supreme value: "There is nothing better than peace in which an end is put to the warfare of things in heaven and earth." (Eph. 4:2).[26]

Lastly, the bishop of Antioch gives mention to both the peace of Christ within and external peace in his opening address to the Trallians: "Ignatius, also called Theophorous, to the holy church at Tralles in Asia, loved by God the Father of Jesus Christ; elect and an honor to God; enjoying inward and outward peace through the Passion of Jesus Christ, who is our hope when we rise to be with Him." (Trall. Intro.).[27]

Peace as a divine gift from Christ, peace as a goal of the Christian life, and peace as the fruition of interior peace into a social peace—all these themes of peace present in the Gospels and the Apostlic Fathers converge with the message of peace attributed to "Mary, Queen of Peace".

Summary Statement

In examining the Gospels of Jesus Christ in the New Testament and the writings of the Apostlic Fathers, one can find the presence of all six foundational themes that arise from the content of the message of Medjugorje. From the presence of the foundational themes in the Gospels, one can conclude that the calls to faith, prayer, fasting, penance, conversion, and peace all have a solid grounding in that source of Divine Revelation inspired by the Holy Spirit and written by the evangelists as sanctified channels of the truth of Christ.

The presence of the identical six themes in the writings of the Apostlic Fathers further illustrates that these six calls and their implementation was a resolute concern of the earliest Christian community, those Christians who had personal exposure to the apostles of Christ and their immediate successors.

Let us proceed, then, to an examination of the developmental content of the message of Medjugorje in relation to the Documents of Vatican Council II and the contemporary, post-conciliar statements of the official teaching body of the Catholic Church (Magisterium).

Notes
Chapter Three

[1] All scripture citations will be taken from the *Holy Bible: Revised Standard Version*, Catholic Edition, London, C.T.S., 1966, unless otherwise noted.

[2] Francis X. Glimm, tr., *The Fathers of the Church*, Vol. 1, New York, C.I.M.A., 1947, p. 37.

[3] James A. Kleist, S.J., tr., *Ancient Christian Writers*, Vol. 1, Maryland, Newman Press, 1961, p. 65.

[4] *Ibid.*, p. 66.

[5] Glimm, *Fathers*, pp. 183-184.

[6] Kleist, *Writers*, p. 84.

[7] Cf. Glimm, *Fathers*, p. 184.

[8] Kirsopp Lake, tr., *The Apostolic Fathers*, Vol. 1, Cambridge, Harvard University Press, 1947, p. 321.

[9] Kleist, *Writers*, p. 96.

[10] *Ibid.*, p. 64.

[11] This passage taken from *New American Bible: Catholic Edition*, Catholic Biblical Association of America, 1970.

[12] Glimm, *Fathers*, p. 177.

[13] Lake, Fathers, p. 309. Cf. Mt. 5:11.

[14] Glimm, *Fathers*, p. 177.

[15] Note: *The Shepherd of Hermas* (c. 140-150 A.D.) offers an entire treatise on the discipline of penance in apocalyptic form, but according to J. Quasten and other contemporary patrologists, this writing rightfully belongs to the apocryphal apocalypses and the Apostolic Fathers. Cf. Quasten, *Patrology*, Vol. 1, p. 13.

[16] Kleist, *Writers*, p. 43.

[17] Kleist, *Writers*, pp. 13-14. Old Testament passages: Ez. 33:11-27; Is. 1:15-20.

[18] *Ibid.*

[19] *Ibid.*, p. 22.

[20] *Ibid.*, p. 64.

[21] Cf. *supra*, Chapter I, section 2.

[22] Luke 13:24.

[23] Kleist, *Writers*, p. 21.

[24] *Ibid.*, p. 24. Old Testament passages: Ps. 33:12-18; Ps. 31:10.

[25] *Ibid.*

[26] Glimm, *Fathers*, p. 92.

[27] Kleist, *Writers*, p. 75.

CHAPTER IV

Presence of the Medjugorje Developmental Content in the Documents of Vatican Council II and Post-Conciliar Documents

The fourteen developmental themes that arise out of the individual Medjugorjian messages, as presented in Chapter II, will here be examined as to their mutual presence in the documents of Vatican Council II and in post-conciliar documents. These products of the Magisterium of the Catholic Church represent an exercise of the official teaching authority of the Church in its function of presenting the two-fold source of Sacred Scripture and Sacred Tradition in a contemporary and authentic formulation of Divine Revelation.

Jesus Christ—The One Redeemer and Mediator

The attestation of the single role of Jesus Christ as Redeemer of the world, and as sole Mediator of the world to the Father as found in the message of Medjugorje is also clearly present in the documents of the Second Vatican Council. The Constitution on the Sacred Liturgy (*Sacrosantum Concilium*, Dec. 4, 1963) begins by establishing Jesus Christ as the Word made flesh, sent by the Father as the divinely ordained Mediator between God and man:

> God who "wills that all men be saved and come to the knowledge of truth" (1 Tim. 2:4), "who in many times and in various ways spoke of old to the fathers through the prophets" (Heb. 1:1), when the fullness of time had come, sent his Son, the Word made flesh, anointed by the Holy Spirit, to preach the gospel to the poor, to heal the contrite of heart, to be a bodily and spiritual medicine: the Mediator between God and Man.[1]

The role of Jesus Christ as "He who redeemed the world on the cross" as contained in the Medjugorjian message, is also present in the *Constitution on the Sacred Liturgy*, where the redemptive effort of Christ is described as being foreshadowed in the Old Testament and achieved in the midst of the paschal mystery:

The wonderful words of God among the people of the Old Testament were but a prelude to the work of Christ our Lord in redeeming mankind and giving perfect glory to God. He achieved this task principally by the paschal mystery of his blessed passion, resurrection from the dead, and glorious ascension, whereby "dying, he destroyed our death, and rising, restored our life."[2]

The Vatican II Decree on the Church's Missionary Activity (*Ad Gentes Divinitus*, December 7, 1965), refers to Christ as the one Mediator who gave His life as a ransom for many for the salvation of mankind, which denotes a salvific message that must be preached to the ends of the earth:

Jesus Christ was sent into the world as the true Mediator between God and men . . . the Son of Man did not come to be served, but to serve and to give his life as a ransom for many, that is for all (cf. Mk. 10:45). . . . Now, what was once preached by the Lord or fulfilled in Him for the salvation of mankind, must be preached and spread to the ends of the earth (Acts 1:8), starting from Jerusalem (cf. Lk. 24:27), so that what was accomplished for the salvation of all men may, in the course of time, achieve its universal effect.[3]

The post-conciliar document issued by the Magisterium that most clearly presents the role of Jesus Christ as sole redeemer and mediator is the 1979 encyclical of Pope John Paul II, *Redemptor Hominis* (On the Redemption of Humanity). The opening line of the encyclical offers a profound statement in regard to Christ as Redeemer and center of human history: "The Redeemer of Man, Jesus Christ, is the center of the universe and of history."[4]

In his discussion of the mystery of Redemption, Pope John Paul II asks the question as to the manner in which the Church should continue its fundamental mission of leading the faithful to salvation. His answer, an echo of the answer seen in the message of Medjugorje, points to the sole redeemer and source of salvation:

To the question, dear Brothers, sons and daughters, a fundamental and essential response must be given. Our response must be: Our spirit is set in one direction, the only direction for our intellect, will and heart is towards Christ, the Redeemer of Man. We wish to look towards him because there is salvation in no one else but him the Son of God repeating what Peter said: "Lord, to whom shall we go? You have the words of eternal life".[5]

The Pope continues by describing Christ as the sole mediator to the Father who adequately satisfied the fatherhood of God, and the Redeemer of all creation who enables fullness of justice to reach all human hearts through the Heart of the First-born Son:

. . . Jesus Christ, the Son of the living God, became our reconciliation with the Father. He it was, and He alone, who satisfied the Father's eternal love, that fatherhood that from the beginning found expression in creating the world, giving man all the riches of creation, and making him "little less than God", in that he was created "in the image and after the likeness of God." He and He alone satisfied the fatherhood of God and that love which man in a way rejected by breaking the first Covenant and the later covenants that God "again and again offered to man." The redemption of the world—this tremendous mystery of love in which creation is renewed—is, at its deepest root, the fullness of justice in a human Heart—the Heart of the First-born Son—in order that it may become justice in the hearts of many human beings, predestined from eternity in the first-born Son to be children of God and called to grace, called to love.[6]

Finally, John Paul II summarizes the twofold role of Christ as sole redeemer and mediator to the Father, two Christological themes at the heart of the message of Medjugorje, in this passage that exclaims the value of humanity that would call for the labors of so great a Redeemer:

How precious must man be in the eyes of the Creator, if he "gained so great a Redeemer," and if God "gave his only Son" in order that man "should not perish but have eternal life."[7]

Renewal in the Holy Spirit

The central role of the Holy Spirit in the foundation, mission, and spiritual revitalization of the Church is an essential doctrine of the faith, and a recurring theme in the Medjugorjian message. The Dogmatic Constitution on the Church (*Lumen Gentium*, November 21, 1964) attests to the role of the Holy Spirit in the continual sanctification of the Church, the indwelling of the Holy Spirit in the hearts of the faithful, the bestowal of various hierarchical and charismatic gifts, and the instant renewal of the Church through the Holy Spirit:

When the work which the Father gave the Son to do on earth (cf. Jn. 17:4) was accomplished, the Holy Spirit was sent on the day of Pentecost in order that he might continually sanctify the Church, and that, consequently, those who believe might have access through Christ in one Spirit to the Father (cf. Eph. 2:18). He is the Spirit of Life, the fountain of water springing up to eternal life (cf. Jn. 4:47; 7:38-39). To men, dead in sin, the Father gives life through him, until the day when, in Christ, he raises to life their mortal bodies (cf. Rom. 8:10-11). The Spirit dwells in the Church and in the hearts of the faithful, as in a temple (cf. 1 Cor. 3:16; 6:19). Guiding the Church in the way of truth (cf. Jn. 16:13) and unifying her in communion and in the works of ministry, he bestows upon her varied hierarchic and charismatic gifts, and in this way directs her; and he adorns her with his fruits (cf. Eph. 4:11-12, 1 Cor. 12:4; Gal. 5:22). By the power of the Gospel he permits the Church to keep the freshness of youth. Constantly he renews her and leads her to perfect union with her Spouse. For the Spirit and the Bride both say to Jesus, the Lord: "Come!" (cf. Apoc. 22:17).

The Decree on the Church's Missionary Activity further defines the crucial task of the Holy Spirit in the life of the Church, as it is likewise attested to in the Medjugorjian content, being the very soul of the Church and at times anticipating the Church in her apostolic action:

> Through the ages the Holy Spirit makes the entire Church "one in communion and ministry"; and provides her with different hierarchical and charismatic gifts, "giving life to ecclesiastical structures, being as it were their soul, and inspiring in the hearts of the faithful that same spirit of mission which impelled Christ himself. He even at times anticipates apostolic action, just as in various ways he unceasingly accompanies and directs it.[9]

Pope Paul VI in his encyclical on Evangelization in the Modern World (*Evangelii Nuntiandi*, December 8, 1975) discusses the vital tasks of the Holy Spirit in regard to the promulgation of the Gospel of Jesus Christ to all nations. In the light of the truth that it is the Holy Spirit that makes evangelization possible, Pope Paul VI refers to the renewed sense of the Holy Spirit within the Church, and the call for all heralds of the Gospel (the responsibility of all Christians) to pray unceasingly to the divine Spirit, abandoning ourselves to His guidance:

> We see in the Church today an age dominated, as it were, by the Holy Spirit. The faithful are striving everywhere, not merely to know and understand him better as he is revealed in Holy Scripture, but also to surrender themselves to him with joyous hearts, opening their minds to his inspiration. They assemble in great numbers in His honor. They are eager to be guided by Him. . . . The faithful who have received the seal of the Holy Spirit in baptism should study in greater depth the nature and the manner of the activity of the Holy Spirit in evangelization in these times. This is our desire and we urge all the heralds of the Gospel, whatever be their order of rank, to pray unceasingly to the divine Spirit with faith and ardor and to submit themselves prudently to his guidance. . . .[10]

A final attestation to the need of unceasing prayer and renewal in the Holy Spirit called for at Medjugorje appears in *Cathechesi tradendae*, the 1979 exhortation by Pope John Paul II on Catechesis in Our Time. Here the Holy Father discusses the instrumentality of the Holy Spirit in the effort of every catechist, and the call to an authentic "renewal in the Spirit":

> To invoke the Spirit constantly, to be in communion with him, to endeavor to know his authentic inspirations must be the attitude of the teaching Church and of every catechist.
>
> Secondly, the deep desire to understand better the Spirit's action and to entrust himself to him more fully . . . must bring about a catechetical awakening. For "renewal in the Spirit" will be authentic and will have real fruitfulness in the Church, not so much according as it gives rise to extraordinary charisms, but according as it leads the greatest number of the

faithful, as they travel their daily paths, to make a humble, patient and persevering effort to know the mystery of Christ better and better, and to bear witness to it.[11]

Hence, the sanctifying role of the Holy Spirit in the life of the Church is not to be underestimated. For that which is the soul of the Church demands the prayer and praise of the faithful fitting for the Third Person of the Trinity, in His mission of *continually* renewing the spiritual life of the Church.

Mary—Universal Mother and Intercessor

As maintained in the Medjugorjian message, the Council Fathers present Mary's twofold role as univeral Mother of all humanity and as intercessor for the world in the Dogmatic Constitution on the Church (*Lumen Gentium*, November 21, 1964). Describing Mary's motherhood in the order of grace, the Council Fathers refer to Mary's singular cooperation with the labors of Christ in restoring humanity to the possibility of supernatural life:

> She conceived, through faith, and nourished Christ, she presented him to the Father in the Temple, shared her Son's sufferings as he died on the cross. Thus, in a wholly singular way she cooperated by her obedience, faith, hope, and burning charity in the work of the Savior in restoring supernatural life to souls. For this reason she is a mother to us in the order of grace.[12]

The document continues to establish the motherhood of Mary after her assumption into Heaven, where her office of intercession for the wayfaring brethren of her Son continues, but which neither adds to nor subtracts from the office of her Son as the one Mediator:

> This motherhood of Mary in the order of grace continues—uninterruptedly from the consent she loyally gave at the Annunciation and which she sustained without waivering beneath the cross, until the eternal fulfillment of the elect. Taken up to Heaven, she did not lay aside this saving office but by her manifold intercession continues to bring us the gifts of eternal salvation. By her maternal charity, she cares for the brethren of her Son, who still journeys on earth surrounded by dangers and difficulties, until they are led into their blessed home. Therefore the Blessed Virgin is invoked in the Church under the title of Advocate, Helper, Benefactress and Mediatrix. This, however, is so understood that it neither takes away from nor adds anything to the dignity and efficacy of Christ the one Mediator.[13]

The Dogmatic Constitution on the Church further exemplifies the use of Mary's intercessory role for humanity in ending the Marian section of

the constitution by prayerfully invoking the Mother of Christ and men for
the union of all peoples by the spiritual bond of peace:

> The entire body of the faithful pours forth urgent supplications to the
> Mother of God and of men that she, who aided the beginnings of the Church
> by her prayers, may now, exalted as she is above all the angels and saints,
> intercede before her Son in the fellowship of all the saints until all families
> of people, whether they are honored with the title of Christians or whether
> they still do not know the Savior, may be happily gathered together in peace
> and harmony into one People of God, for the glory of the Most Holy and
> Undivided Trinity.[14]

In the apostolic exhortation, *Marialis Cultus* (To Honor Mary, February
2, 1974), Pope Paul VI calls the Christian world to a renewal of devotion
to Mary, Mother of the Church. He further explicates Mary's role of
spiritual Motherhood as the intercessory means of Christian unity:

> Just as at Cana the Blessed Virgin's intervention resulted in Christ per-
> forming his first miracle (cf. Jn. 2:1-12), so today her intercession can help
> to bring to realization the time when the disciples of Christ will again find
> full communion in faith. This hope of ours is strengthened by a remark of
> our predecessor Leo XIII, who wrote the cause of Christian unity "Properly
> pertains to the role of Mary's spiritual Motherhood."[15]

It is also interesting to note that in this Marian document Pope Paul VI
instituted the World Day of Peace to be celebrated on the Feast Day of
Mary, the Mother of God, January 1st. The Pope speaks of the fittingness
of the unity of these two themes, Mary, the Mother of God, and Peace (as
is strongly accentuated in the Medjugorjian message) in calling for a
renewed adoration of the Prince of Peace, who offers His supreme gift of
peace through "Mary, Queen of Peace":

> It [Feast of Mary, the Mother of God] is meant also to exalt the singular
> dignity which this mystery brings to the "Holy Mother . . . through whom
> we were found worthy to receive the Author of Life". It is likewise a fitting
> occasion for renewing adoration to the newborn Prince of Peace, for
> listening once more to the glad tidings of the angels (cf. Lk. 2:14), and for
> imploring from God through the Queen of Peace, the supreme gift of
> peace.[16]

Finally, Pope John Paul II reinforces the exceptional character of the
Motherhood of Mary and her intercessing participation in the salvation of
humanity, in the encyclical *Redemptor Hominis*:

> Nobody has been brought into it (the mystery of Redemption) by God
> himself as Mary has. It is in this that the exceptional character of the grace
> of divine Motherhood consists. Not only is the dignity of this Motherhood
> unique and unrepeatable in the history of the human race, but Mary's
> participation, due to this Maternity, in God's plan for man's salvation
> through the mystery of the Redemption is also unique in profundity and
> range of action.[17]

Mary's role as mother of humanity and as universal intercessor, through which man is to receive the peace of Christ, constitute Medjugorjian themes firmly rooted in the contemporary teachings of the Magisterium.

Mass and Eucharistic Adoration

The need for Christians to participate in the holy sacrifice of the Mass, as requested in the message of Medjugorje, is clearly stated in the Constitution on the Sacred Liturgy. The document calls the faithful to participate in the Mass in all its respective aspects of assistance:

> They [the faithful] should be instructed by God's word, and be nourished at the table of the Lord's Body. They should give thanks to God. Offering the Immaculate Victim, not only through the hands of the priest but also together with him, they should learn to offer themselves through Christ, the Mediator, they should be drawn day by day into ever more perfect union with God and each other, so that finally God may be all in all.[18]

In the Instruction on the Worship of the Eucharistic Mystery (*Eucharistic Mysterium*, May 25, 1967), issued shortly after the Council, the adoration of the Blessed Sacrament is established as a valid practice of the faithful (paralleling the Medjugorjian call to "adore the most Holy Sacrament of the Altar"): "The practice of adoration has a valid and firm foundation, especially since belief in the Real Presence of the Lord has as its natural consequence the external and public manifestation of that belief."[19]

The document goes on to describe the immense benefits of visitation of the Blessed Sacrament as a means of union with Christ dwelling within: "The devotion which leads the faithful to visit the Blessed Sacrament draws them into an ever deeper participation into the Paschal Mystery. . . . Dwelling with Christ our Lord, they enjoy His intimate friendship and pour out their hearts before Him for themselves and their dear ones, and pray for the peace and salvation of the world."[20]

A later document by the Church's Magisterium in April, 1980, Instruction on Certain Norms Concerning the Worship of the Eucharistic Mystery (*Inaestimabile Donum*) sustains the call of the faithful to participate in Eucharistic adoration. The section of the document pertaining to Eucharistic worship outside of Mass states: "Public and private devotion to the Holy Eucharist outside Mass also is highly recommended: for the presence of Christ, who is adored by the faithful in the Sacrament, derives from the sacrifice and is directed towards sacramental and spiritual communion."[21]

Lastly, Pope John Paul II describes the unequalled earthly union with Christ attainable in the reception of the Sacrament of Holy Eucharist in the encyclical *Redemptor Hominis*: "The Eucharist is the most perfect Sacrament of this union. By celebrating and also partaking of the Eucharist we unite ourselves with Christ on earth and in Heaven who intercedes with and for us with the Father, but we always do so through the redeeming act of His sacrifice, through which he redeemed us, so that we have been 'bought with a price.' "[22]

Sacramental Confession

The Sacrament of Confession, whereby reconciliation with Christ and forgiveness of sins is received through the absolution given by the priest, is a call present in the content of the Medjugorjian messages and in the teaching of the Church's Magisterium. In 1974, the document introducing the New Order of Penance (*Misericordiam Suam*) speaks of the necessity of sacramental Confession, in particular for the forgiveness of grave sin:

> Those who depart from the fellowship of the love of God through grave sin are recalled through the Sacrament of Penance to the life which they had lost. Those who fall into venial sin, however, experiencing their weakness daily, receive through frequent Confession the strength to arrive at the full freedom of the children of God.
> The God of Mercy laid down that, in order to receive the saving remedy of the Sacrament of Penance, the Christian should confess to a priest all and every grave sin which he can recall after an examination of his conscience.[23]

The document continues to speak of frequent Confession and its spiritual fruits, but cautions against a merely ritual, repetitional use of the sacrament (in a manner very similar to the reprimand of Mary in the reported messages in regard to a mechanical, merely habitual participation in sacramental Confession):[24] "Further, frequent and reverent recourse to this sacrament, even when only venial sins are in question, is of great value. Frequent Confession is not mere ritual repetition, nor is it a mere psychological exercise. Rather it is a constant effort to bring to perfection the grace of our baptism. . . ."[25]

Reconciliatio et Paenitentia, the post-synodal exhortation of John Paul II issued on December 2, 1984, places the Sacrament of Confession in the mainstream of the Christian call to reconciliation and penance. His first fundamental conviction in regards to the Sacrament of Penance is to focus on it as the ordinary, Christ-instituted means to receive the forgiveness of sins, and hence calls every Christian to its use:

> The first conviction is that, for a Christian, the Sacrament of Penance is the ordinary way of obtaining forgiveness and the remission of serious sins committed after Baptism. . . . In the school of faith we learn that the same Savior desired and provided that the simple and precious Sacraments of

faith would ordinarily be the effective means through which His redemptive power passes and operates. It would therefore be foolish, as well as presumptuous, to wish arbitrarily to disregard the means of grace and salvation which the Lord has provided. . . .[26]

As is exemplified in the Medjugorjian call to at least monthly Confession, the Holy Father also makes reference to the contemporary crisis that the Sacrament of Confession is experiencing, and calls for its renewal and reaffirmation:

It is good to renew and reaffirm this faith [in the Sacrament of Penance] at a moment when it might be weakening, losing some of its completeness or entering into an area of shadow or silence, threatened as it is by the negative elements in the above-mentioned crisis. For the Sacrament of Confession is indeed being undermined. . . . A further negative influence is the routine of a sacramental practice sometimes lacking in fervour and real spontaneity, deriving perhaps from a mistaken and distorted idea of the effects of the Sacrament. It is therefore appropriate to recall the principal aspects of this great Sacrament.[27]

The Rosary

The Magisterial call to the recitation of the Rosary as a prayer and meditation on the mysteries of Christ and His Mother can clearly be seen in the 1974 Apostolic Exhortation, *Marialis Cultus*. Pope Paul VI begins by referring to the long line of papal predecessors who have encouraged and invited the faithful to pray the Rosary:

We wish now, venerable Brothers, to dwell for a moment on the renewal of the pious practice which has been called "the compendium of the entire Gospel": the Rosary. To this our predecessors have devoted close attention and care. On many occasions they have recommended its frequent recitation, encouraged its diffusion, explained its nature, recognized its suitability for fostering contemplative prayer—prayer of both praise and petition—and recalled its intrinsic effectiveness for promoting Christian life and apostolic commitment.[28]

Paul VI continues to describe the Rosary as a meditational prayer on the principal salvific events accomplished by Christ and the final events of the life of Mary:

The Rosary considers in harmonious succession the principal salvific events accomplished by Christ, from his Virginal Conception and the mysteries of his childhood to the culminating moments of the Passover—the blessed Passion and the glorious Resurrection—and the effect of this on the infant Church on the day of Pentecost; and on the Virgin Mary when at the end of her earthly life she was assumed body and soul into her heavenly home.[29]

Further, the Christological focus of the Rosary is affirmed by Paul VI as a Gospel prayer whose litany-like succession of Hail Marys become a continual praise of Christ—the final object of the Angel's announcement and the greeting of Elizabeth:

> As Gospel prayer, centered on the mystery of the redemptive Incarnation, the Rosary is therefore a prayer with a clearly Christological orientation. Its most characteristic element, in fact, the litany-like succession of Hail Marys, becomes in itself an unceasing praise of Christ, who is the ultimate object both of the Angel's announcement and of the greeting of the Mother of John the Baptist: "Blessed is the fruit of your womb." (Lk. 1:42).[30]

A final re-emphasis of the call to Christians to pray the Rosary is evident in John Paul II's *Familiaris Consortio*. Particularly in regard to the recitation of the Family Rosary, another call accentuated in the message of Medjugorje, the Holy Father speaks of the strong insistence with which the Church proposes its recitation (quoting Pope Paul VI from *Marialis Cultus*):

> While respecting the freedom of the children of God, the Church has always proposed certain practices of piety to the faithful with particular solicitude and insistence.
>
> Among these should be mentioned the recitation of the Rosary: "We now desire, as a continuation of the thought of our predecessors, to recommend strongly the recitation of the Family Rosary. . . . There is no doubt that . . . the Rosary should be considered as one of the best and most efficacious prayers in common that the Christian family is invited to recite. We like to think, and sincerely hope, that when the family gathering becomes a time of prayer, the Rosary is a frequent and favored manner of praying."[31]

Renewal of Sacred Scripture

A renewal in the reading, praying, and meditating upon Sacred Scripture on a daily basis as requested in the message of Medjugorje, also possesses a grounding in the contemporary teachings of the Magisterium. The Dogmatic Constitution on Divine Revelation (*Dei Verbum*, November 18, 1965) discusses the central role of Sacred Scripture in the life of the Church, calling for the continual nourishing of the faithful by the divine word:

> She [the Church] has always regarded, and continues to regard, the Scriptures, taken together with Sacred Tradition, as the supreme rule of her faith. For, since they are inspired by God and committed to writing once and for all time, they present God's own Word in an unalterable form, and they make the voice of the Holy Spirit sound again and again in the words of

the prophets and apostles. It follows that all the preaching of the Church, as indeed the entire Christian religion, should be nourished and ruled by Sacred Scripture. . . . Access to Sacred Scripture ought to be open wide to the Christian faithful.[32]

Dei Verbum also attests to the primacy of the Gospels among all inspired writings, coinciding with the Medjugorjian emphasis on the Gospels:

It is common knowledge that among all the inspired writings, even among those of the New Testament, the Gospels have special place, and rightly so, because they are our principal source for the life and teaching of the Incarnate Word, our Saviour.[33]

The Vatican II Document on Divine Revelation ends with a renewed call to the reading and studying of the sacred books, leading to a new impulse of the spiritual life of the Church:

So that it may come that, by the reading and studying of the sacred books ''the Word of God may speed on in triumph'' (2 Th. 3:1) and the treasure of Revelation entrusted to the Church may more and more fill the hearts of men. Just as firm, constant attendance at the Eucharistic mystery the life of the Church draws increase, so a new impulse of the spiritual life may be expected from increased veneration of the Word of God, which ''stands forever.''[34]

The Medjugorjian call to ''implant the divine word in our hearts'' as seen in a message transmitted by Jelena[35] is an invitation also extended by the Sacred Congregation for Religious and Secular Institutes in its 1981 document, *La plenaria* (The Contemplative Dimension of Religious Life). This document calls all the faithful, and especially those in religious life, to have a daily encounter with the Word of God through listening and meditation:

Listening to and meditating on the Word of God is a daily encounter with the ''surpassing knowledge of Jesus Christ'' (PC 6; ES II, 16, 1). The Council ''warmly and insistently exhorts all the Christian faithful, especially those who live the religious life, to learn this sublime knowledge (DV 25).[36]

Devotion to the Sacred Heart of Jesus and the Immaculate Heart of Mary

On the anniversary of the second centenary of the institution of the Feast of the Sacred Heart of Jesus (February 6, 1965), Pope Paul VI issued the Apostolic Letter, *Investigabiles Divitias Christi* that proclaims devotion to the Sacred Heart an excellent form of sanctioned piety. The Pope states the desire that the infinite riches of the Sacred Heart is paid due honor by all the faithful:

We desire that the deep and intrinsic doctrinal foundations which throw light upon the infinite treasures of love the Sacred Heart be explained to all the faithful in an adapted and complete manner, and that special ceremonies be organized for the purpose of developing ever more the devotion to the cult which deserves the highest consideration to the end that all the faithful, moved by a new spirit, pay due honor to the divine Heart. . . .[37]

Pope Paul VI continues by establishing devotion to the Sacred Heart of Jesus as one of those popular devotions discussed by the Vatican Council as highly recommended because of its worthy adoration and reparation offered to Jesus Christ:

Since the venerable Ecumenical Council highly recommends "popular devotions of Christian people . . . above all when they are ordered by the Apostlic See" (Constitution on the Sacred Liturgy, n. 13), this form of devotion seems to impose itself in a particular way. For as mentioned above, it insists essentially in worthily adoring Jesus Christ and offering him reparation; it is based above all on the Sacred mystery of the Eucharist from which, as from all other liturgical actions, flow "the sanctification of men in Christ and the glorification of God, to which all other activities of the Church are directed as to their end."[38]

Dives in Misericordia, the encyclical of John Paul II in 1980 on the Mercy of God, offers a further impetus for devotion to the Sacred Heart of Jesus in this passage, which points to the Heart of Christ as a focal point in the mercy of God:

The Church seems in a particular way to profess the mercy of God and to venerate it when she directs herself to the Heart of Christ. In fact, it is precisely this drawing close to Christ in the mystery of His Heart which enables us to dwell on this point—a point in a sense central and almost more accessible on the human level—of the revelation which instituted the central content of the messianic mission of the Son of Man.[39]

The Medjugorjian call for devotion to the Immaculate Heart of Mary, juxtaposed with its call to devotion to the Sacred Heart of Jesus, is also present in the Magisterial documents, as seen in John Paul II's reference to the maternal heart of Mary in the encyclical *Redemptor Hominis*:

We can say that the mystery of the Redemption took shape beneath the heart of the Virgin of Nazareth when she pronounced her "fiat". From then on, under the special influence of the Holy Spirit, this heart of both a Virgin and a Mother, has always followed the words of her Son and has gone out to all those whom Christ has embraced and continues to embrace with inexhaustible love. For that reason, her heart must also have the inexhaustibility of a Mother. The special characteristic of the Motherly love that the Mother of God inserts in the mystery of the Redemption and the life of the Church finds expression in its exceptional closeness to man and all that happens to him. It is in this way that the mystery of the Mother exists.[40]

The same Pope continues to discuss the heart of Mary and its merciful, maternal love for humanity in his document, *Dives in Misericordia*:

It was precisely this "merciful" love, which is manifested above all in contact with moral and physical evil, that the heart of her who was the Mother of the Crucified and Risen One shared in singularly and exceptionally—that Mary shared in. In her and through her this love continued to be revealed in the history of the Church and of humanity. This revelation is especially fruitful because in the Mother of God it is based upon the unique fact of her maternal heart, on her particular sensitivity, on her particular fitness to reach all those who most easily accept the merciful love of a Mother.[41]

Pope John Paul II has also exemplified the validity and the efficacy of devotion to the Hearts of Jesus and Mary, firstly by issuing a family prayer of consecration to the Sacred Heart and the Immaculate Conception, December 8, during the 1983 Holy Year of Redemption; and secondly by his formal consecration of the world to the Immaculate Heart of Mary on the Feast of the Annunciation, March 25, 1984 during the same Holy Year.

Finally, the turning to both the Hearts of Jesus and Mary as signs of mercy, reconciliation, and love is specifically called for in the recent encyclical of John Paul II, *Reconciliatio et Paenitentia* (December 2, 1984). In this document, the Pontiff invites the faithful to the turning to the Heart of Christ, to foster a greater hatred of sin, and a greater conversion to God, our source of peace and reconciliation:

In order that in the not too distant future abundant fruits may come from it, I invite you all to join me in turning to Christ's Heart, the eloquent sign of Divine Mercy, the "propitiation for our sins", "Our peace and reconciliation", that we may draw from it an interior encouragement to hate sin and to be converted to God, and find in it the Divine kindness which lovingly responds to human repentance.[42]

The Medjugorjian calls to penance and conversion, effected through the intercession of Mary's Immaculate Heart, are profoundly expounded in this recent papal document. This is visible in the following passage, pointing to the turning to the Immaculate Heart of Mary, in whom the reconciliation of God and man is effected through the necessary path of penance:

I likewise invite you to turn with me to the Immaculate Heart of Mary, Mother of Jesus in whom "is effected the reconciliation of God with humanity, . . . is accomplished the work of reconciliation, because she has received from God the fullness of grace in virtue of the redemptive sacrifice of Christ.

Into the hands of this Mother . . . to her Immaculate Heart—to which we have repeatedly entrusted the whole of humanity, disturbed by sin and tormented by so many tensions and conflicts—I now in a special way entrust this intention: that through her intercession humanity may discover and travel the path of penance, the only path that can lead it to full reconciliation.[43]

Hence, the call to consecrate and entrust oneself to the Sacred Heart of Jesus and Immaculate Heart of Mary lies firmly rooted in the official statements of the post-conciliar Pontiffs as well as the messages attributed to Mary at Medjugorje.

Heaven, Purgatory, Hell, and Satan

The reality of Heaven, Purgatory, and Hell, oftentimes downplayed in contemporary Catholic education, preaching, and evangelization, is accentuated in the message of Medjugorje as an active reality that demands a vital response in this life. An attestation to the fundamental reality of these forms of afterlife is also visible in the May 29, 1979 document issued by the Sacred Congregation for the Doctrine of the Faith, *The Reality of Life After Death*. Precisely in the light of contemporary lack of fidelity to these truths, the document unambiguously states the reaity of Heaven and Hell, and the possible need of souls to enter Purgatory:

> In fidelity to the New Testament and Tradition, the Church believes in the happiness of the just who will one day be with Christ. She believes that there will be eternal punishment for the sinner, who will be deprived of the sight of God, and that this punishment will have a repercussion on the whole reality of the sinner. She believes in the possibility of a purification for the elect before they see God, a purification altogether different from the punishment of the damned.[44]

The same reality is stated in the profession of faith issued by Pope Paul VI as *The Credo of the People of God* (June 30, 1968). In his introductory words, the Pontiff calls attention to the lack of acceptance of the fullness of the Catholic doctrines of faith by contemporary Catholics, the passion for doctrinal novelty, and its result in the confusion of the faithful:

> In making this profession, we are well aware of the disquiet in matters of faith which is unsettling some of the convictions of our contemporaries. . . . We see even Catholics possessed by what is almost a passion for change and novelty. . . . The greatest care must be taken that the important duty of research does not involve the undermining of the truths of the Christian doctrine. If this happens—and we have unfortunately seen it happen in these days—the result is the perplexity and confusion in the minds of many of the faithful.[45]

Paul VI then proceeds by proclaiming, as part of the credo, the belief in eternal life for the souls who die in Christ, and the existence of Purgatory as a possible transition of expiation:

> We believe in eternal life. We believe that the souls of all those who die in the grace of Christ—whether they must still make expiation in the fire of

Purgatory, or whether from the moment they leave their bodies they are received by Jesus into Paradise like the good thief—go to form that People of God which succeeds death, death which will be totally destroyed on the day of the Resurrection when these souls are reunited with their bodies.[46]

Satan, his existence and continual effort to lead humanity away from Christ as seen in the Medjugorjian message, can also be found in the document on Demonology Magisterially commissioned in 1975, *Christian Faith and Demonology*. The document, strongly recommended by the Sacred Congregation as a sure means for the faithful in grasping the teaching of the Church on Satan and his activity, attests to the reality of the devil and the need to defend oneself from his efforts:

> . . . The Church is simply being faithful to the example of Christ when it asserts that the warning of St. Peter to be "sober" and alert is always relevant. In our day, we must indeed defend ourselves against a new "intoxication" with Satan. . . .[47] When a doubt is thrown these days on the reality of the devil we must, as we observed earlier, look to the constant and universal teaching of the Church and to its chief source, the teaching of Christ. It is in the teaching of the Gospel and in the heart of the faith as lived that the existence of the world of demons is revealed as a dogma.[48]

This document also speaks, in a manner similar to the words of Mary in the ability of prayer to disarm Satan,[49] of the importance of faith that opens the heart to prayer in the victory over the devil:

> It is, in fact, to faith that St. Peter the Apostle appeals when he urges us to resist the devil as men "solid in your faith". Faith tells us that evil is "a living, spiritual being that is perverted and perverts others. . . . Faith opens the heart to prayer, wherein it finds its triumph and crown, for prayer wins for us the victory over evil, thanks to God's grace.[50]

Ecumenism

Respect for all authentic religions, dismissing unnecessary segregation, upholding the truth that the Holy Spirit does not preside equally in all religions, maintaining that Jesus Christ is the one and only Mediator to the Father, and stating that the divisions of the one religion are man-made, comprise the substance of the ecumenical message of Medjugorje.[51] The same guidelines for proper Christian relations to non-Christian religions appear in the Conciliar Document, *Nostrae Aetate* (Declaration on the Relation of the Church to Non-Christian Religions, October 28, 1965).

After discussing the elements of truth and high moral conduct visible in several of the major world religions, the Council Fathers established the singularity of Christ as the way, the truth, and the life:

The Catholic Church rejects nothing of what is true and holy in these religions. She has a high regard for the manner of life and conduct, the precepts and doctrines which, although differing in many ways from her own teaching, nevertheless often reflect a ray of that truth which enlightens all men. Yet She proclaims and is in duty bound to proclaim without fail, Christ who is the way, the truth, and the life (Jn. 1:6). In Him, in whom God reconciled all things to Himself (2 Cor. 5:18-19), men find the fullness of their religious life.[52]

Further, the Medjugorjian statement that the presence of the Holy Spirit does not preside equally in every church coincides with the constant teaching of the Magisterium that the Catholic Church is the one true Church of Christ in its fullness of sanctification by the Spirit, as stated here in *Lumen Gentium*:

This is the sole Church of Christ which in the Creed we profess to be one, holy, Catholic and apostolic. . . . This Church, constituted and organized as a society in the present world, subsists in the Catholic Church, which is governed by the successors of Peter and by the bishops in communion with him. Nevertheless, many elements of sanctification and of truth are found outside its visible confines. Since these are gifts belonging to the Church of Christ, they are forces impelling towards Catholic unity.[53]

The Council Fathers continue by urging a prudent integration of dialogue and collaboration with members of other faiths: "The Church, therefore, urges her sons to enter with prudence and charity into discussion and collaboration with other religions. Yet Christians, while witnessing to their own faith and way of life, acknowledge, persevere, and encourage the spiritual and moral truths found among non-Christians, also their social life and culture."[54]

In regard to affecting unity between the Catholic Church and other separated Christian communities, the Conciliar Decree on Ecumenism (*Unitatis Redintegratio*, November 21, 1964) calls for the restoration of all Christians, and refers to the human-made, and not Christ-made divisions amidst Christianity as a reflection of the Medjugorjian message:

The restoration of unity among all Christians is one of the principal concerns of the Second Vatican Council. Christ the Lord founded one Church and one Church only. However, many Christian communities present themselves to me as the true inheritors of Jesus Christ; all indeed profess to be followers of the Lord but they differ in mind and go their different ways, as if Christ Himself were divided. Certainly, such division openly contradicts the will of Christ, scandalizes the world, and damages the holy cause, the preaching of the Gospel to every creature.[55]

Finally, the post-conciliar document *Ecumenical Collaboration at the Regional, National and Local Levels* issued by the Secretariat for the Promotion of Christian Unity in 1975 stresses that it is by way of the "local Church" in every respective town or city that ecumenical efforts are to be undertaken: "From the Catholic perspective ecumenical responsibilities of the local Church emerge clearly. . . . Therefore the local Church . . . can be in a very favorable position to make contact and establish fraternal relations with other Christian churches and communicate at these levels."[56]

Hence, it is evident that the Magisterium likewise is calling all parishes, whether they be placed in large metropolitan cities or in a small village town such as Medjugorje, to a greater respect, dialogue and prudent integration with those who do not share in the fullness of Christian truth and faith.

Family and Community Prayer

The theme of family and community prayer in the message of Medjugorje reflects a strong post-conciliar movement that has its basis in the teaching of the Magisterium. For example, the greater appearance of youth prayer groups and its fruitfulness to the Church is attested to by Pope John Paul II's catechetical exhortation of 1979, *Catechesi Tradendae*:

> I may also mention the youth groups that, under varying names and forms but always with the purpose of making Jesus Christ known and of living the Gospel, are in some areas multiplying and flourishing in a sort of spring-time that is very comforting to the Church: these include Catholic Action groups, charitable groups, prayer groups, and Christian meditational groups. These groups are a source of great hope for the Church of tomorrow.[57]

A further affirmation of the fruits of Christians coming together to pray in a singular, unified voice is found in the 1978 document *Mutuae Relationes*: "Today, by the disposition of divine providence, many of the faithful are led to gather into small groups to hear the Gospel, to meditate in depth and practice contemplation. . . . It is indispensible to make certain that all, above all pastors, give themselves to prayer. . . ."[58]81

The specific request for family prayer finds its best magisterial formulation in the encyclical *Familiaris Consortio*. John Paul II describes the particular characteristics of family prayer and its fruits for the "domestic Church":

> Family prayer has its own characteristic qualities. It is prayer offered in common, husband and wife together, parents and children together. . . . The words which the Lord Jesus promises his presence can be applied to the members of the Christian family in a special way: "Again I say to you, if two of you agree on earth about anything they ask it will be done for them by My Father in heaven. For where two or three are gathered in my Name, there am I in the midst of them."[59]

The Pontiff continues by stating that the proper dignity and responsibility of the family can be achieved through their prayers in common petition: "The dignity and responsibility of the Christian family as the domestic Church can be achieved only with God's unceasing aid, which will surely be granted if it is humbly and trustingly petitioned in prayer."[60]

Finally, John Paul II exhorts the family to the Family Rosary, quoting his predecessor Paul VI:

> There is no doubt that . . . the Rosary should be considered as one of the best and most efficacious prayers in common that the Christian family is invited to recite. We like to think, and sincerely hope, that when the family gathering becomes a time of prayer, the Rosary is a frequent and favoured manner of praying." In this way authentic devotion to Mary . . . constitutes a special instrument for nourishing loving communion in the family and for developing conjugal and family spirituality.[61]

Offering of Sufferings and Sacrifices

The spiritual practice of offering all sufferings and sacrifices endured, is a discipline called for in the content of the Medjugorjian message. While particular spiritual practices would not be highlighted in Magisterial statements by their very nature, one finds reference to the efficacy of the offering of one's daily trials and sufferings, beginning in *Lumen Gentium*. In the chapter on the laity, the Council Fathers speak of the daily events of the Christian life, and in particular trials patiently endured, as comprising offerings pleasing to the Father when done "in the Spirit": "For all their works, prayer, and apostolic undertakings, family and married life, daily work, relaxation of mind and body, if they are accomplished in the Spirit—indeed even the hardships of life if patiently borne—all these become spiritual sacrifices acceptable to God through Jesus Christ" (cf. Pet. 2:5).[62]

Further, the Council Fathers state that it is in the celebration of the Eucharist, along with the offering of His own Son that these spiritual sacrifices are most acceptable to the Father: "In celebration of the Eucharist these [sacrifices] may most fittingly be offered to the Father along with the Body of the Lord.[63]

Salvifici Doloris, the 1984 Apostolic Letter on the Christian Meaning of Human Suffering written by Pope John Paul II, makes specific reference to the practice of offering one's suffering to God, which will effect a more rapid union of humanity into "one":

> And so there should come together in spirit beneath the Cross on Calvary all suffering people who believe in Christ, and particularly those who suffer because of their faith in Him who is the Crucified and Risen One, so that the

offering of their sufferings may hasten the fulfillment of the prayer of the Saviour Himself that all may be one.[64]

The Pope profoundly explains the fruits of the offering of human suffering in its mysterious "completion" of the sufferings of Christ, as once inexhaustible and infinite and yet open to all love expressed in human suffering:

> Insofar as man becomes a sharer in Christ's sufferings—in any part of the world and at any time in history—to that extent *he in his own way completes* the suffering through which Christ has accomplished the Redemption of the world.
>
> Does that mean that the Redemption achieved by Christ is not complete? No. It only means that the Redemption, accomplished through satisfactory love, *remains always open to all love expressed in human suffering. . . .* Yes, it seems part of the very essence of Christ's redemptive suffering that this suffering requires to be unceasingly completed.[65]

Finally, John Paul II points to Mary as the preemptive example of one who shared in the sufferings of Christ, and through her compassion offers a unique contribution to suffering in patient endurance and obedience to the will of the Father:

> . . . It was on Calvary that Mary's suffering, beside the suffering of Jesus, reached an intensity which can hardly be imagined from a human point of view . . . . As a witness to her Son's Passion by her presence, and as a sharer in it by her compassion, Mary offered a unique contribution to the Gospel of suffering. . . . She truly has a special title to be able to claim that she "completes in her flesh"—as already in her heart—"what is lacking in Christ's afflictions."[66]

Abandonment to God

Regarding the request contained in the message of Medjugorje to "abandon yourselves" to God, the conciliar and post-conciliar documents refer to the same type of abandonment to God that fosters full trust, reliance, and submission to the divine workings in our lives, while at the same time upholding the Christian responsibility to actively fulfill the commandments of God. *Dei Verbum* (the Dogmatic Constitution on Divine Revelation) speaks of the entire commitment of self to God that flows from a viable Christian faith: "By faith man freely commits his entire self to God, making 'the full submission of his intellect and will to God. . . .' "[67]

Abandonment to the Holy Spirit, as also requested in the message of Medjugorje, is a contemporary reality in the call to offer oneself completely to God, as seen in Paul VI's document, *Evangelii Nuntiandi*:

"The faithful are striving everywhere, not merely to know and understand him [the Holy Spirit] better . . . but also to surrender themselves to him with joyous hearts, opening their minds to his inspiration. They are eager to be guided by him."[68]

The 1971 document issued by the Sacred Congregation on the Clergy in regard to catechetics, *General Catechetical Directory*, describes a proper docility to the Holy Spirit as one which always includes the living out of the commandments of God and the laws of the Church, and not an abandonment that rids one of the obligations of Christian moral life:

> "The love of God has been poured out in our heart through the Holy Spirit which has been given to us" (Rom. 5:5). Docility to the Holy Spirit implies also the faithful observance of God's commandments, of the laws of the Church, and of just civil laws.[69]

Lastly, the same post-conciliar document denotes a commitment of one's entire self made through a free obedience of faith to God's manifest will:

> Men and women are called to obey the will of God freely in all things. This is "the obedience of faith by which people freely commit their entire selves to God." (DV 5).[70]

Eschatological Urgency

The strand of urgency for the conversion of humanity present in the message of Medjugorje can likewise be found in the post-conciliar teachings of the Magisterium, particularly in the encyclicals of Pope John Paul II.

The first encyclical of his pontificate, *Redemptor Hominis*, alludes to an all too soon yielding of the effects of what modern man is producing by his hands and his mind, leading humanity to live increasingly in fear:

> The man of today seems to be under the threat from what he produces, that is to say from the result of the works of his hands and, even more so, of the work of his intellect and the tendencies of his will. All too soon, and often in an unforeseeable way, what this manifold activity of man yields . . . turns against man himself. . . . This seems to make up the main chapter of the drama of present-day human existence in its broadest and universal dimension. Man therefore lives increasingly in fear.[71]

Further, the Pope speaks of man's material advancements as praiseworthy, but as a means to man himself being dominated and manipulated by failing to remember his God-originated dominion (a statement quite similar to Mary's description of the West):[72] "Indeed there is already a real percepted danger that, while man's dominion over the world of things is making enormous advances, he should lose the essential threads of his dominion and in various ways, let his humanity be subjected to manipulation of the world. . . ."[73]

The Pontiff further speaks of the eschatological faith in the Church that allows it to be a prophet of the most important signs of our times:

> Inspired by eschatological faith, the Church considers an essential, unbreakable united element of her mission this solicitude for men. . . . She finds the principle of this solicitude in Jesus Christ Himself, as the Gospel witnesses. This is why she wishes to make it grow continually through her relationship with Christ, reading man's situation in the modern world in accordance with the most important signs of our time.[74]

In the 1980 encyclical *Dives in Misericordia*, On the Mercy of God, the same strand of urgency of conversion and need for God's mercy in regard to the contemporary evil in the world can be traced, as in this passage concerning the critical nature of our present age: "however, at no time and in no historical period—*especially at a moment as critical as our own*—can the Church forget the prayer that is a cry for the mercy of God amid the many forms of evil which weigh upon humanity and threaten it."[75]

A pointed statement as to the possible victory of evil in the world and the need for a "new flood" to account for sins of humanity appears in the same document: ". . . Like the prophets, let us appeal to that love which has maternal characteristics and which, like a mother, follows each of her children, each lost sheep, even if they should number millions, even if in the world evil should prevail over goodness, even if contemporary humanity should deserve a 'new flood' on account of its sins. . . ."[76]

The Pope continues by imploring God's mercy, as a servant of Christ, for humanity in this hour of human history, which, in echo of the message of Medjugorje, may be approaching an "immense danger":

> And if any of our contemporaries does not share the faith and hope which lead me, as a servant of Christ and steward of the mysteries of God, to implore God's mercy for humanity in this hour of history, let him at least try to understand the reason for my concern. It is dictated by love for man, for all that is human and which, according to the intuitions of many of our contemporaries, is threatened by an immense danger.[77]

John Paul II proceeds to state his obligation to beg for the mercy of God for this difficult and critical phase of the history of the Church and of the world: "The mystery of Christ . . . also obliges me to proclaim mercy as God's merciful love. . . . It likewise obliges me to have recourse to that mercy and to beg for it in this difficult, critical phase of the history of the Church and of the world, as we approach the end of the second millenium."[78]

In the 1984 Apostolic Exhortation, *Reconciliatio et Paenitentia*, Pope

John Paul II quotes the consoling words from St. Peter in invoking Christian hope and peace in combatting sin in the world, and the fruits of suffering in doing God's will in this critical period of human history:

> At an hour of history which is no less critical, I dare to join my exhortation to that of the Prince of the Apostles, the first to occupy this See of Rome as a witness to Christ and as a Pastor of the Church. . . . "Have unity of spirit. . . . Be zealous for what is right." and he added: "It is better to suffer for doing right, if that should be God's will, than for doing wrong."[79]

Finally, so that "in the not too distant future" the Church may bear great fruit, the Pontiff invites all to turn to the Heart of Christ, sign of peace, reconciliation, conversion, and repentence:

> In order that in the not too distant future abundant fruits may come from it, I invite you all to join me in turning to Christ's Heart, the eloquent sign of divine mercy, the "propitiation for our sins," "our peace and reconciliation" that we may all draw from it inter-encouragement to hate sin and to be converted to God, and find in it the divine kindness which lovingly responds to human repentence.[80]

Summary Statement

That all fourteen developmental themes that arise from the content of the message of Medjugorje can find their parallel in the conciliar and post-conciliar documents of the Magisterium, leads to two basic conclusions. First, the developmental content of the message of Medjugorje reflects a contemporary, post-conciliar, authentic embodiment of Catholic doctrine. The fact that the developmental themes of the message, when juxtaposed to the most contemporary development of the teaching of the Magisterium, reflect an essential convergence, establish these developmental themes as an up-dated formulation of authentic Catholic teaching. Second, apart from its presence in the content of the message of Medjugorje, the faithful are called to an observance of the before-mentioned elements of the Christian life. Since the themes are deeply rooted in the Church's Magisterial teaching, all Catholics are called by this very fact to the faithful acceptance of these sound Christian directives.

Notes
Chapter Four

[1] Austin Flannery, O.P., ed., *Vatican Council II: The Conciliar and Post-Conciliar Documents*, New York, Costello Publishing Co., 1975, *Sacrosanctum Concilium (SC)*, No. 5, p. 3.

[2] *Ibid., SC*. No. 5, p. 3.

[3] *Ibid., Ad Gentes Divinitus (AD)*, No. 3, p. 815.

[4] Pope John Paul II, Encyclical Letter, *Redemptor Hominis (RH)*, Vatican Polyglot Press, 1979, No. 1.

[5] *Ibid.*, No. 7.

[6] *Ibid.*, No. 9.

[7] *Ibid.*, No. 10.

[8] Flannery, *Vatican II, Lumen Gentium (LG)*, No. 4, p. 351.

[9] *Ibid, AGC*, No. 4, p. 817.

[10] Austin Flannery, O.P., ed., *Vatican II: More Post-Conciliar Documents*, Vol. II, Michigan, Eerdmans Publishing Co., 1982, *Evangelii Nuntiandi (EN)*, No. 75, pp. 750-751.

[11] *Ibid., Catechesi Tradendae (CT)*, No. 72, p. 809.

[12] Flannery, *Vatican II, LG*, No. 61, p. 418.

[13] *Ibid., LG*, No. 62, p. 419.

[14] *Ibid., LG*, No. 69, p. 423.

[15] Pope Paul VI, *Marialis Cultus*, Vatican Polyglot Press, 1974, No. 33.

[16] *Ibid.*, No. 5.

[17] John Paul II, *RH*, No. 22.

[18] Flannery, *Vatican II, SC*, No. 48.

[19] *Ibid., Eucharisticum Mysterium (EM)*, No. 49, p. 129.

[20] *Ibid.*, No. 50, p. 130.

[21] Flannery, *Post-Conciliar Documents, Inaestimabile Donum (ID)*, No. 20, p. 98.

[22] John Paul II, *RH*, No. 20.

[23] Flannery, *Post-Conciliar Documents, Misericordiam Suam (MS)*, No. 7, p. 39.

[24] Cf. *supra*, Chapter I, section 6.

[25] Flannery, *Post-Conciliar Documents, MS*, No. 7, p. 39.

[26] John Paul II, *Reconciliatio et Paenitentia (RP)*, Vatican Polyglot Press, 1974, No. 42.

[27] *Ibid.*, No. 28.

[28] Paul VI, *Marialis Cultus*, Vatican Polyglot Press, 1974, No. 42.

[29] *Ibid.*, No. 45.

[30] *Ibid.*, No. 46.

[31] John Paul II, *Familiaris Consortio (FC)*, No. 61.

[32] Flannery, *Vatican II, Dei Verbum (DV)*, Nos. 21, 22, p. 762.

[33] *Ibid., DV*, No. 18, p. 760.

[34] *Ibid., DV*, No. 25, p. 765.

[35] Cf. *supra*, Chapter 2, section 6.

[36] Flannery, *Post-Conciliar Documents, La Plenaria (LP)*, No. 8, p. 248.

[37] Paul VI, *Investigabiles Divitias Christi* as found in T. O'Donnell, *Devotion to the Heart of Jesus*, Rome, Institute of Spirituality, Angelicum, p. 209.

[38] *Ibid.*

[39] *Ibid.*, John Paul II, *Dives in Misericordia (DM)*, No. 13.

[40] *Ibid., RH*, No. 22.

[41] *Ibid., DM*, No. 9.

[42] John Paul II, *RP*, No. 35.

[43] *Ibid.*

[44] Flannery, *Post-Conciliar Documents, The Reality of Life After Death*, S.C.D.F., p. 502.

[45] Flannery, *Post-Conciliar Documents, CREDO*, p. 388.

[46] *Ibid., CREDO*, p. 394.

[47] Flannery, *Post-Conciliar Documents, Christian Faith and Demonology*, S.C.D.W., p. 477.

[48] *Ibid.*, p. 476.

[49] Cf. *supra*, Chapter I, section 8.

[50] Flannery, *Post-Conciliar Documents, Demonology*, p. 478.

[51] Note: This is to speak of ecumenism in its broadest sense, as including relations of the faithful to members of non-Christian religions, as well as seeking the unity of all Christians.

[52] Flannery, *Vatican II, Nostrae Aetate (NA)*, No. 2, p. 739.

[53] *Ibid., LG*, No. 8, p. 357.

[54] *Ibid.*

[55] *Ibid., Unitatis Redintegratio (UR)*, No. 1, p. 452.

[56] Flannery, *Post-Conciliar Documents, Reunis a Rome*, p. 158.

[57] *Ibid., CT*, No. 47, p. 790.

[58] *Ibid., Mutue Relationes (MR)*, S.C.R.S.I., No. 16, p. 221.

[59] John Paul II, *Familiaris Consortio*, No. 59.

[60] *Ibid.*

[61] *Ibid.*, No. 61.

[62] Flannery, *Vatican II, LG*, No. 34, p. 391.

[63] *Ibid.*

[64] John Paul II, *Salvifici Doloris (SD)*, Vatican Polyglot Press, 1984, No. 31.

[65] *Ibid.*, No. 24.

[66] *Ibid.*, No. 25.

[67] Flannery, *Vatican II, DV*, No. 5, p. 752.

[68] Flannery, *Post-Conciliar Documents, EN*, No. 75, p. 750.

[69] *Ibid., General Catechetical Directory*, No. 63, p. 565.

[70] *Ibid., GCD.*, No. 64, p. 566.

[71] John Paul II, *RH*, No. 15.

[72] Cf. *supra*, Chapter I, section 2.

[73] John Paul II, *RH*, No. 16.

[74] *Ibid.*, No. 15.

[75] John Paul II, *DM*, No. 15.

[76] *Ibid.*

[77] *Ibid.*

[78] *Ibid.*

[79] John Paul II, *RP*, No. 35.

[80] *Ibid.*

CHAPTER V

The Message of Medjugorje in Relation to the Messages of Lourdes and Fatima

The apparitions of the Blessed Virgin Mary at Lourdes, France in 1858, and at Fatima, Portugal in 1917, have been ecclesiastically approved for belief and devotion by the faithful.* Both these Marian apparitions were accompanied by messages, words spoken by Mary to the respective visionaries, that called for a response, the nature of which reports have to have a significant effect on the course of human history.

The message of Medjugorje likewise comprises a call that claims to possess a global significance for humanity. How does the urgent call to humanity found in the Medjugorje message attributed to Mary, "Queen of Peace" compare with the calls present in the messages of Lourdes and Fatima made by the "Immaculate Conception" and "Our Lady of the Rosary"? The relationship between the message of Medjugorje and these two earlier messages from the Blessed Virgin Mary will here be examined, with a particular emphasis upon the common thematic strands possessed in the three messages, and the nature of development also observable between the three message contents.

---

* Private revelation consists of a supernatural manifestation of Christian truth made after the close of public revelation (Sacred Scripture and Tradition) with the death of the last apostle. The Church can give her "negative approval" to a private revelation or apparition by stating that there is nothing contained in it that is contrary to faith and morals. In approving an apparition or a revelation, the Church does not intend to guarantee that authenticity of the respective private revelation, but states that the content of the apparition can be accepted by the faithful without any doctrinal danger in regard to faith and morals.

Yet, it is considered reprehensible if after the Church has given her negative approval of a private revelation, any member of the faithful were to contradict or ridicule the revelation. Further, if after prudent judgement, it has been personally determined that a given revelation is authentic, the one who has received the revelation should accept it in the spirit of faith, and if the private revelation contains any message for others, those persons also have an obligation to accept the truth of the revelation and act upon it. Cf. J. Aumann, O.P., *Spiritual Theology*, London, Sheed and Ward, 1979, p. 429.

The Message of Lourdes

Bernadette Soubirous (born January 7, 1844), illiterate village girl from Lourdes, France, received eighteen apparitions of the Blessed Virgin Mary between February 11, 1858 and July 16, 1858. The following is an account of the eighteen apparitions and the concurrent messages reported by the fourteen-year-old Bernadette.

First Apparition, February 11, 1858: The first apparition received by Bernadette was accompanied by no verbal message, but did contain references to the recitation of the Rosary. Here is Bernadette's account of the first apparition:

> . . . I saw a Lady dressed in white, she was wearing a white dress and a blue sash and a yellow rose on each foot the color of the chain of her rosary. . . . I put my hand in my pocket, I found my Rosary in it, I wanted to make the sign of the cross, I could not get my hand up to my forehead; it fell back, the vision made the sign of the cross, then my hand shook, I tried to make it and I could, I said my Rosary, the vision ran the beads of hers through her fingers but she did not move her lips, when I had finished my Rosary, the vision disappeared all of a sudden. . . .[1]

Second Apparition, February 14, 1858: The second apparition was accompanied by Bernadette sprinkling holy water upon the "lady", to which Mary (in an identical response to the sprinkling of holy water performed by Vicka in Medjugorje) smiled in return: "And I did see her as I threw the water at her; she smiled at me and nodded her head; when I finished saying my beads she disappeared. . . ."[2]

Third Apparition, February 18, 1858: Bernadette had been instructed by a local townswoman, Mmd. Milhet, to ask the lady to write down her name with pen and paper on a portable writing desk. The following is the exchange between Bernadette and "Aqueró" (literally, "That", as Bernadette referred to her):

Bernadette:	Will you have the goodness to put your name in writing?
Mary:	(smiling) That isn't necessary.
Mary:	Will you be kind enough to come here for a fortnight?
Bernadette:	Yes.
Mary:	I don't promise to make you happy in this world, but in the next.[3]

Fourth Apparition, February 19, 1858: The fourth apparition was without any verbal message. The only report in reference to this apparition attested to the deep ecstasy experienced by Bernadette observed by seven or eight townspeople who were present.[4]

Fifth Apparition, February 20, 1858: The fifth apparition, at approximately 6:00 a.m., was also without a publicly revealed message. The apparition lasted for fifteen minutes.[5]

Sixth Apparition, February 21, 1858: This report of the sixth apparition comes from Dr. Dozous, medical doctor at Lourdes and eyewitness. Dozous reports the following change in Bernadette's facial expressions and the rationale given for the change by Bernadette:

> As soon as she had come before the grotto, Bernadette knelt down, took out of her pocket her Rosary and began to pray, saying her beads. Her face underwent a perfect transformation noticed by all who were near, and showed that she was *en rapport* with the Appearance. . . . Soon I saw her face, which until then had expressed the most perfect joy, grow sad; two tears fell from her eyes and rolled down her cheeks. This change occurring in her face during her station surprised me. I asked her, when she had finished her prayers and the mysterious being had disappeared, what had passed within her during this long station. She answered: "The Lady, walking away from me for a moment, directed her glance afar, above my head. Then looking down upon me again, she said, 'Pray for the sinners.' I was quickly reassured by the expression of goodness and sweetness which I saw return to her face, and immediately she disappeared."[6]

Seventh Apparition, February 23, 1858: Although the seventh apparition of Mary was accompanied by a dialogue, Bernadette never revealed the contents of the conversation. There is speculation that it was during this apparition that Mary taught Bernadette a special prayer to be said by Bernadette every day of her life but not to be divulged; or it may have been the apparition where Bernadette received three secrets from Mary that were also to remain private. The secrets were revealed to Bernadette with the directive: "I forbid you to repeat this to anyone."[7]

Eighth Apparition, February 24, 1858: The dialogue between Mary and Bernadette on the day of the eighth apparition has also not been revealed completely, but portions of the dialogue have been reported. During the apparition, Bernadette, in tears, turned to the on-lookers and distinctly said, "Penitence, Penitence, Penitence!", words Bernadette heard from the lips of "Aquero".[8] Mary also said: "You're to pray to God for sinners."[9] Bernadette further reported that Mary had requested her to go up the slope of the cave on her knees and "kiss the ground in penance for the conversion of sinners" to which Bernadette immediately complied.[10]

Ninth Apparition, February 25, 1858: The ninth apparition was accompanied by instructions to perform acts of penance (*i.e.*, eating grass) and to "drink from the spring", a directive which resulted in Bernadette's digging, uncovering the miraculous spring at Lourdes known throughout the world for its cures. The following is Bernadette's account:

. . . While I was in prayer, the Lady said to me in a friendly, but serious voice, "Go, drink and wash in the spring." As I did not know where this spring was, and as I did not think the matter important, I went towards the river. The Lady called me back and signed to me with her finger to go under the grotto to the left; I obeyed but I did not see any water. Not knowing where to get it from, I scratched the earth and the water came. I let it get a little clear of the mud, then I drank and washed.[11]

Upon being questioned as to the reason for eating the grass, Bernadette replied: "I do not know. The Lady urged me by an inner impulse." Bernadette was further reported to have been saying to herself during her acts of penance, "Penitence! Penitence!"[12]

Tenth Apparition, February 27, 1858: Similar penitential exercises were performed by Bernadette, namely walking on her knees, drinking the water from the new spring, and washing her face in the muddy water. The only words reported from this tenth appearance were found in this account from a witness:

Upon her arrival at the Grotto, Bernadette without any hesitation passed by the place which she usually occupied and knelt down at the top of the slope at the point where she had scratched the earth the day before. She showed no surprise at finding the new spring flowing and, having crossed herself, drank and washed there. Having dried her face with the corner of her apron, she returned to the back and knelt down upon the stone which served her for a *prie-dieu*. She entered immediately into communication with Her who was the joy of her soul, reciting the Rosary with devotion and self-abandonment, when the well-loved voice in a tone of sadness spoke to her these words: "You will kiss the earth for sinners." . . . Not satisfied with having responded personally to the Lady's request, she wished to associate everyone with herself in the work of reparation. She turned towards the crowd and with a gesture of her hand ordered everyone present to bow face downwards to the ground. As if the order had come directly from the mouth of the Lady herself, every knee was bent and every head touched for a moment the soil of the grotto. Those who could not bow so low as the ground placed their kiss of penitence upon parts of the rock.[13]

Eleventh Apparition, February 28, 1858: The only words recorded from the dialogue between Our Lady and Bernadette regarded instructions from Mary to have a chapel built at the grotto. The message was directed to the parish priests, as seen in this account by the witness Jean-Pierre Estrade:

At the end of their conversation the Lady, so the seer told us, seemed to be thinking deeply; when she emerged from her reflections she said to her little protégée, "Go and tell the priests that a chapel must be built here."[14]

Twelfth Apparition, March 1, 1858: No message accompanied the twelfth apparition and Bernadette's ordinary penitential exercises, except for the incident of the "borrowed Rosary". Bernadette had been lent a

Rosary by a local woman, and took it from her pocket to begin her usual prayers during the apparition, at which point Aqueró instructed her to return that particular Rosary to her pocket, and to use her own Rosary.[15]

Thirteenth Apparition, March 2, 1858: Besides the regular penitential exercises, Bernadette was reported to have had a lengthy and animated conversation with Mary, but the only words revealed from the conversation were the following regarding the instruction to have people come to the grotto in procession (instructions again directed to the parish priest): "Go and tell the priests that people are to come here in procession."[16]

Fourteenth Apparition: March 3, 1858: At Bernadette's first visit to the grotto that day, and reciting her expected Rosary, no apparition took place. Later that same day, Bernadette returned to the grotto, and received a brief apparition. The only message revealed was a repeated request to the parish priest for the construction of a chapel at the site.[17]

Fifteenth Apparition, March 4, 1858: The fifteenth apparition, the last in the fortnight of visits requested by Mary, was comprised of an appearance which lasted approximately forty-five minutes, during which Bernadette is reported to have smiled thirty-four times and bowed twenty-four times.[18] After the apparition ended, Bernadette was immediately questioned as to whether there was any message to be conveyed, and as to whether this end of the requested fortnight would also mean the end of the apparitions. The following eyewitness account presents the response of Bernadette:

> Bernadette remained nearly an hour in ecstasy. . . . As soon as the seer had resumed her normal attitude, the persons near her hastened to ask her how the Lady had left her. "Just as usual," replied the child. "She smiled when she departed but she did not say good-bye to me."[19]

In response to whether Bernadette will return to the grotto in light of the fact that the fortnight was now over, she replied: "Oh yes, I shall. . . . I shall keep coming, but I do not know whether the Lady will appear again."[20]

Sixteenth Apparition, March 25, 1858: After a three-week interlude, a twenty-day time-span marked by an undeniable conversion of the people of Lourdes, who were frequenting sacramental Confession and holy Mass like never before, Mary appeared to Bernadette on the feast of the Annunciation. It was at this sixteenth apparition that the Lady finally answered the question of her identity that she had previously refused to answer. The following is Bernadette's account of the apparition, as recorded by Estrade:

> ". . . When I was on my knees before the Lady," she continued, "I asked her pardon for arriving late. Always good and gracious, she made a sign to me with her head that I need not excuse myself. Then I spoke to her of all

my affection, all my respect and the happiness I had in seeing her again. After having poured out my heart to her I took up my Rosary. While I was praying, the thought of asking her name came before my mind with such persistence that I could think of nothing else. I feared to be presumptuous in repeating a question she had always refused to answer. And yet something compelled me to speak. At last, under an irresistible impulse, the words fell from my mouth, and I begged the Lady to tell me who she was. The Lady did as she had always done before; she bowed her head and smiled but she did not reply. I cannot say why, but I felt myself bolder and asked her again to graciously tell me her name; however she only bowed and smiled as before, still remaining silent. Then once more, for a third time, clasping my hands and confessing myself unworthy of the favour I was asking of her, I again made my request. . . . The Lady was standing above the rose-bush, in a position very similar to that shown in the miraculous medal. At the third request her face became very serious and she seemed to bow down in an attitude of humility. Then she joined her hands and raised them to her breast. . . . She looked up to heaven . . . then slowly opening her hands and leaning forward towards me, she said to me in a voice vibrating with emotion: '*I am the Immaculate Conception!*' ''[21]

Seventeenth Apparition, April 7, 1858: The seventeenth apparition offers Only the added information, by way of content, of Bernadette's continual penance and recitation of the Rosary during the apparition. This fact is attested to in the account of the apparition by Dr. Dozous, where he reports the "candle miracle":

One day when Bernadette seemed to be even more absorbed than usual in the appearance upon which her gaze was riveted, I witnessed, as also did everyone else there present, the fact which I am about to narrate.

She was on her knees saying with fervent devotion the prayers of her Rosary which she held in her left hand while in her right was a large blessed candle alight. The child was just beginning to make the usual ascent on her knees when she suddenly stopped and, her right hand joining her left, the flame of the big candle passed between the fingers of the latter. Though fanned by a fairly strong breeze, the flame produced no effect upon the skin which it was touching. Astonished at this strange fact, I forbade anyone to interfere, and taking my watch in hand, I studied the phenomenon attentively for a quarter of an hour. At the end of this time, Bernadette, still in her ecstasy, advanced to the upper part of the grotto, separating her hands. The flame thus ceased to touch her left hand.

Bernadette finished her prayer and the splendor of the transfiguration left her face. She rose and was about to leave the grotto when I asked her to show me her left hand. I examined it most closely but could not find the least trace of burn anywhere upon it. . . . I record this fact just as I have seen it without attempting to explain it.[22]

Eighteenth Apparition, July 16, 1858: On the feast of Our Lady of Mount Carmel, Bernadette received her last apparition of "Aqueró". In spite of the barricades set up by the municipal authorities around the grotto, Bernadette sensed the inner impulse to return to the surrounding grotto area. The last apparition, here described by Estrade, presents no particular message content apart from the parting ''smiles'' of the Blessed Virgin Mary:

Almost as soon as the child began to look towards the rock on the other side of the river the light of ecstasy transfigured her face and in the transports of her ravished soul she cried, ''Yes, yes, there she is. She welcomes us and is smiling across the barriers!'' Then instantly began between the Virgin and Bernadette that wonderful spiritual communing. . . . During the whole of the vision she continued gracious and smiling and when she quitted her little ecstatic, she left her in the fullness of joy.[23]

The fundamental message conveyed by Mary, the ''Immaculate Conception'' to St. Bernadette in the eighteen Lourdes apparitions and their sparce concurrent messages consists fundamentally of the call to prayer and penance offered to God for the conversion of sinners. Mary's directive to ''pray for the sinners'' in the sixth apparition of February 21, and that of the eighth apparition of February 24, where Mary instructs Bernadette that she ''must pray to God for sinners'' comprise two of the very few directives disclosed by Bernadette. The example of Bernadette in her consistent penitential exercises during the apparitions, the instructions of Our Lady to ''kiss the ground in penance for the conversion of sinners'' during the eighth apparition of February 24, the account of Bernadette repeating the words of Mary, ''Penitence, penitence'', during the same apparition, and the inner impulse that caused Bernadette to eat grass and walk on her knees during the ninth apparition, February 25, illustrate the crucial Lourdes imperative to perform penance for the conversion of sinners and in reparation to God. The recitation of the Rosary also comprises an implicit call in the message of Lourdes, evident both by the fact that Aqueró always appeared with a Rosary in hand, and because of the recitation of the Rosary by Bernadette that took place before, during, and after most apparitions.

Hence, it is the call to prayer (with an emphasis on the Rosary) and penance offered to God for the conversion of sinners that summarizes the message of Lourdes—a succinct but crucial message from the Immaculate Mother of God that attests to the sinfulness of humanity, and the vital need for humanity to return to God through prayer and penance.

The Message of Fatima

The identical call to prayer and penance in reparation to God and for the conversion of sinners contained in the message of Lourdes is found, but with a significantly greater development and specification, in the apparitions and accompanying messages of the 1917 Marian apparitions of Fatima. These ecclesiastically approved apparitions of the Virgin Mary to three young Portuguese shepherd children contain the same call to prayer and penance for world conversion, but offer a more detailed manner by which the world can respond to this salvific request.

The message of Fatima was received by three young shepherd children from the mountain town of Fatima, Portugal: Lucia de Jesus Santos (born March 22, 1907) and her first cousins, Jacinta de Jesus Marto (born March 11, 1910) and Francisco de Jesus Marto (born June 11, 1908).[24] The message of Fatima actually begins with three anticipatory apparitions in 1916 by the Angel who identified himself as the "Angel of Peace".[25] The following is an account of the first angelic appearance taken from the memoirs of Sr. Lucia (written at the request of her Bishop):

> We spent the day there among the rocks, in spite of the fact that the rain was over and the sun was shining bright and clear. We ate our lunch and said our Rosary. . . . Our prayer finished and we started to play "pebbles". We had enjoyed the game for a few moments only, when a strong wind began to shake the trees. We looked up, startled to see what was happening, for the day was unusually calm. Then we saw coming towards us, above the olive trees, the figure I have already spoken about. Jacinta and Francisco had never seen it before, not had I ever mentioned it to them. As it drew closer, we were able to distinguish its features. It was a young man, about fourteen or fifteen years old, whiter than snow, transparent as crystal when the sun shines through it, and of great beauty. On reaching us, he said, "Do not be afraid! I am the Angel of Peace. Pray with me." Kneeling on the ground, he bowed down until his forehead touched the ground, and made us repeat these words three times: "My God, I believe, I adore, I hope and I love you. I ask pardon of you for those who do not believe, do not adore, do not hope and do not love you." Then rising, he said: "Pray thus. The Hearts of Jesus and Mary are attentive to the voice of your supplications."[26]

From the very beginning of the Fatima messages, the call to prayer and penance for those who "do not believe, do not adore, do not hope, and do not love" is apparent. This first message serves as a bridge that doctrinally and thematically continues the Marian message of Lourdes. Later in the same year of 1916 (the exact dates were not recorded), Lucia and her cousins, Jacinta and Francisco, received their second apparition of the Angel of Peace, here described by Lucia in her second memoir:

> Some time passed and summer came, when we had to go home for siesta. One day, we were playing on the stone slabs of the well down at the bottom of the garden belonging to my parents. . . . Suddenly, we saw besides us the same figure, or rather Angel, as it seemed to me. "What are you doing?" he asked. "Pray, pray very much! The most holy Hearts of Jesus and Mary have designs of mercy on you. Offer prayers and sacrifice constantly to the Most High." "How are we to make sacrifices," I asked. "Make of everything you can a sacrifice, and offer it to God as an act of

reparation for the sins by which He is offended, and in supplication for the conversion of sinners. You will thus draw down peace upon your country. I am its Angel Guardian, the Angel of Portugal. Above all, accept and bear with submission, the suffering which the Lord will send you."[27]

The second message from the Angel of Portugal continues the imperative for prayer and penance for reparation to God and the conversion of sinners. But this message begins to specify the manner of fruitful prayer and penance through the offering of any and all sacrifices, for the twofold goal of atonement to God and supplication for sinners. Devotion to the Hearts of Jesus and Mary are again reiterated by the Angel, and peace for the country is stated as a further result of an obedient response to providentially permitted sufferings.

The third and final appearance of the Angel of Peace in preparation for the Marian apparitions to begin the following year, 1917, was the occasion for a Eucharistic apparition where the themes of reparation for sin and conversion of sinners made through the merits of the Hearts of Jesus and Mary, is more greatly accentuated. The following is Lucia's account:

A considerable time had elapsed, when one day we went to pasture our sheep on a property belonging to my parents. . . . As soon as we arrived there, we knelt down, with our foreheads touching the ground, and began to repeat the prayer of the Angel:

"My God, I believe, I adore, I hope, and I love you. . . ." I don't know exactly how many times we had repeated this prayer, when an extraordinary light shone upon us. We sprang up to see what was happening, and beheld the Angel. He was holding a chalice in his left hand, with the Host suspended above it, from which some drops of blood fell into the chalice. Leaving the chalice suspended in the air, the Angel knelt down beside us and made us repeat three times:

"Most Holy Trinity, Father, Son, and Holy Spirit, I offer you the most precious Body, Blood, Soul, and Divinity of Jesus Christ, present in all the tabernacles of the world, in reparation for the outrages, sacrileges, and indifference with which He Himself is offended. And, through the infinite merits of His most Sacred Heart, and the Immaculate Heart of Mary, I beg of you conversion of poor sinners."

Then, rising, he took the chalice and the Host in his hands. He gave the Sacred Host to me, and shared the Blood from the chalice between Jacinta and Francisco,[28] saying as he did so:

"Take and drink the Body and Blood of Jesus Christ, horribly outraged by ungrateful men! Make reparation for their crimes and console your God."

Once again, he prostrated on the ground and repeated with us, three times more, the same prayer, "Most Holy Trinity. . ." and then disappeared.[29]*

---

* The practice of instructing the visionaries by giving them specific prayers to recite, recorded also in the Lourdes apparitions, continues in the Fatima apparitions, and reportedly at Medjugorje.

The strong Eucharistic emphasis in this third and final appearance of the Angel of Peace is presented in the context of reparation, attainable through the offering of the immaculate victim to the most Holy Trinity for the outrages, sacrileges, and indifferences by which the Paschal Lamb Himself is offended. A continued emphasis on the most Sacred Heart of Jesus, source of infinite merits, and the Immaculate Heart of Mary, the channel to those infinite merits, is contained in this third angelic proclamation, along with the continued call to beg for the conversion of sinners. Eucharistic adoration is also introduced in this appearance as a further specification of the Lourdes call to prayer and penance for the conversion of sinners, together with the reception of the Eucharist offered in reparation for the crimes of humanity, and for divine consolation.

Hence, even before the beginning of the Marian apparitions in 1917, the Fatima apparitions of the Angel of Peace have planted the kernel of the message of Lourdes, and allowed it to develop into a more specified, yet consistent call to prayer and penance, requested under the aspects of specified prayers, the offering of sacrifices, the patient endurance of sufferings, the devotion of the Hearts of Jesus and Mary, Eucharistic reception, offering, and adoration. The development and specification of the message of Lourdes, already visible in the anticipatory apparitions of the Angel of Peace in 1916, continues significantly in the messages that accompany the 1917 apparitions of "Our Lady of the Rosary".

First Apparition, May 13, 1917: The first appearance of Mary and the accompanying message takes place during the latter part of World War I, and a climate of political and social turmoil for the country of Portugal. This first message consisting principally in the invitation from Mary to return for six successive months in the same day of the month, also establishes the general request to offer oneself to God and bear His providentially permitted sufferings in an act of reparation to God for the conversion of sinners. The following is Lucia's account of the first apparition (taken from her fourth memoir):

> High up on the slope in the Cova da Iria, I was playing with Jacinta and Francisco at building a little stone wall around a clump of furze. Suddenly we saw what seemed to be a flash of lightning. "We'd better go home," I said to my cousins, "that's lightning; we may have a thunderstorm." "Yes, indeed!" they answered.
>
> We began to do down the slope, hurrying the sheep along towards the road. We were more or less half-way down the slope, and almost level with a large holmoak tree that stood there, when we saw another flash of lightning. We had only gone a few steps further when, there before us on a small holmoak, we beheld a lady all dressed in white. She was more brilliant than the sun, and radiated a light more clear and intense than a crystal glass filled with sparkling water, when the rays of the burning sun shine through it.

We stopped, astounded, before the apparition. We were so close, just a few feet from her, that we were bathed in the light which surrounded her, or rather, which radiated from her. Then Our Lady spoke to us:

"Do not be afraid. I do you no harm."

"Where are you from?"

"I am from heaven."

"What do you want of me?"

"I have come to ask you to come here for six months in succession, on the 13th day, at this same hour. Later on, I will tell you who I am and what I want. Afterwards, I will return here yet a seventh time."*

"Shall I go to Heaven too?"

"Yes, you will."

"And Jacinta?"

"She will go also."

"And Francisco?"

"He will go there too, but he must say many Rosaries."

Then I remembered to ask about two girls who had died recently. They were friends of mine and used to come to my home to learn weaving with the eldest sister.

"Is Maria dos Neves in Heaven?"

"Yes, she is."

"And Amélia?"

"She will be in purgatory until the end of the world."

"Are you willing to offer yourselves to God and bear all the suffering He wills to send you, as an act of reparation for the conversion of sinners?"

"Yes, we are willing."

"Then you are going to have much to suffer, but the grace of God will be your comfort."

As she pronounced these last words, ". . . the grace of God will be your comfort," Our Lady opened her hands for the first time, communicating to us a light so intense that, as it streamed from her hands, its rays penetrated our hearts and the innermost depths of our souls, making us see ourselves in God. . . . Then, moved by an interior impulse that was also communicated to us, we fell on our knees, repeating in our hearts:

"O most Holy Trinity, I adore you! My God, my God, I love you in the most Blessed Sacrament."

After a few moments, Our Lady spoke again:

"Pray the Rosary every day, in order to obtain peace for the world, and the end of the war."

Then she began to rise serenely, going up towards the east, until she disappeared in the immensity of space.[30]

Second Apparition, June 13, 1917: Mary's second appearance to the three young Portuguese children continues to speak of the importance of the daily Rosary, and explicitly introduces the desire of Christ for a world-wide devotion to the Immaculate Heart of Mary. Here is the account by Lucia of the second apparition:

* The "seventh time" is a reference to the apparition to Lucia on December 10, 1925, calling for a devotion to the Immaculate Heart of Mary, which will be presented following the six apparitions of 1917.

As soon as Jacinta, Francisco and I had finished praying the Rosary, with a number of other people who were present, we saw once more the flash reflecting the light which was approaching (which we called lightning). The next moment, Our Lady was there on the holmoak, exactly the same as in May.

"What do you want of me?" I asked.

"I wish you to come here on the 13th of next month, to pray the Rosary every day, and to learn to read. Later, I will tell you what I want."

I asked for the cure of a sick person.

"If he is converted, he will be cured during the year."

"I would like to ask you to take us to heaven."

"Yes. I will take Jacinta and Francisco soon. But you are to stay here for some time longer. Jesus wishes to make use of you to make me known and loved. He wants to establish in the world devotion to my Immaculate Heart. I promise salvation to those who embrace it, and those souls will be loved by God like flowers placed by me to adorn His throne."[31]

"Am I to stay here alone?" I asked, sadly.

"No, my daughter. Are you suffering a great deal? Do not lose heart. I will never forsake you. My Immaculate Heart will be your refuge and the way that will lead you to God."

As Our Lady spoke these last words, she opened her hands and for the second time she communicated to us the rays of that same light, as it were, immersed in God. Jacinta and Francisco seemed to be in that part of the light which rose towards Heaven, and I in that which was poured out upon the earth. In front of the palm of the Lady's right hand was a heart encircled by thorns which pierced it. We understood that this was the Immaculate Heart of Mary, outraged by the sins of humanity, and seek reparation.[32]

The message of the second apparition offers a considerable contribution to the development of the fundamental Marian call to prayer and penance for reparation and conversion. Here Mary states that it is the wish of Christ that His Mother is more greatly known and more greatly loved throughout the world, to be specifically promulgated through a world devotion to His Mother's Immaculate Heart, symbol both of her maternal love for all humanity and for the pains suffered by that maternal Heart from the outrages committed against her by the very objects of her love, her earthly children. The message goes on to present her Immaculate Heart as a spiritual refuge in the midst of a temporal suffering and hardship. Mary accentuates the role of her Immaculate Heart as having essentially a role of intercession, as a Christ-intended path bringing the wayfarer to salvation, and never as a devotion that poses the Immaculate Heart as its own final goal.

Further, Mary reveals in this second apparition the image of her Immaculate Heart, the twofold sign of maternal love and maternal suffering as an effect of the actions of humanity. In a much later report by Sister Lucia in 1930, she stated the following specifications as to the five principal types of offenses that constitute blasphemies committed against the Immaculate Heart of Mary (as revealed to her by Christ during an extraordinary experience of his divine presence): 1. blasphemies against the Immaculate Conception; 2. blasphemies against her virginity; 3. blasphemies against her divine motherhood, refusing at the same time to acknowledge her as Mother of men; 4. those who publicly attempt to instill in the hearts of children indifference, contempt, or even hatred of her Immaculate Heart; and 5. Those who insult her directly in her venerated statues and images.[33] Hence the significance of the piercing of the Heart of Mary, prophecised in the Gospels by Simeon at the Presentation, points to a reality that continues to be experienced by the Mother of humanity.

Third Apparition, July 13, 1917: The apparition of July 13 conveys a pivotal contribution in the ongoing development of the Marian message. In this message Mary not only grants the young seers a vision of Hell, but also specifies the principal intention of establishing a world devotion to the Immaculate Heart of Mary, and the means by which it is to be established. Here is the message of that third apparition in the words of Lucia:

A few moments after arriving at the Cova da Iria, near the holmoak, where a large number of people were praying the Rosary, we saw the flash of light once more, and a moment later Our Lady appeared on the holmoak.

"What do you want of me?" I asked.

"I want you to come here on the 13th of next month, to continue to pray the Rosary every day in honour of Our Lady of the Rosary, in order to obtain peace for the world and the end of the war, because only she can help you."

"I would like to ask you to tell us who you are, and to work a miracle so that everybody will believe that you are appearing to us."

"Continue to come here every month. In October, I will tell you who I am and what I want, and I will perform a miracle for all to see and believe."*

I then made some requests, but I cannot recall now just what they were. What I do remember is that Our Lady said it was necessary for such people to pray the Rosary in order to obtain these graces during the year. And she continued:

"Sacrifice yourselves for sinners, and say many times, especially whenever you make some sacrifice: O Jesus, it is for love of You, for the conversion of sinners, and in reparation for the sins committed against the Immaculate Heart of Mary."

As Our Lady spoke these last words, she opened her hands once more, as she had done during the two previous months. The rays of light seemed to penetrate the earth, and we saw, as it were, a sea of fire. Plunged in this fire

* At the request of Lucia for a miracle that would prove the authenticity and foster belief in the apparitions, Mary replies that she will in fact perform a miracle for all to see and believe, but at the end of the apparitions, both of which constitute elements present in the Medjugorjian phenomena.

were demons and souls in human form, like transparent burning embers, all blackened or burnished bronze, floating about in the conflagration, now raised into the air by the flames that issued from within themselves together with great clouds of smoke, now falling back on every side like sparks in huge fires, without weight or equilibrium, amid shrieks and groans of pain and despair, which horrified us and made us tremble with fear. (It must have been this sight which caused me to cry out, as people say they heard me.) The demons could be distinguished by their terrifying and repellent likeness to frightful and unknown animals, back and transparent like burning coals. Terrified and as if to plead for succour, we looked up at Our Lady, who said to us, so kindly and so sadly:

"You have seen Hell where the souls of poor sinners go. To save them, God wishes to establish in the world devotion to my Immaculate Heart. If what I say to you is done, many souls will be saved and there will be peace. The war is going to end; but if people do not cease offending God, a worse one will break out during the pontificate of Pius XI. When you see a night illuminated by an unknown light, know that this is the great sign given you by God that he is about to punish the world for its crimes, by means of war, famine, and persecutions of the Church and of the Holy Father.

"To prevent this, I shall come to ask for the consecration of Russia to my Immaculate Heart, and the Communion of Reparation on the First Saturdays. If my requests are heeded, Russia will be converted, and there will be peace; if not, she will spread her errors throughout the world, causing wars and persecutions of the Church. The good will be martyred, the Holy Father will have much to suffer, various nations will be annihilated. In the end, my Immaculate Heart will triumph. The Holy Father will consecrate Russia to me, and she will be granted to the world. In Portugal, the dogma of the Faith will always be preserved. . . . Do not tell this to anybody. Francisco, yes, you may tell him.

"When you pray the Rosary, say after each mystery: O my Jesus, forgive us, save us from the fire of hell. Lead all souls to heaven, especially those who are most in need."

After this, there was a moment of silence, and then I asked:

"Is there anything more that you want of me?"

"No, I do not want anything more of you today."

Then, as before, Our Lady began to ascend towards the east, until she finally disappeared in the immense distance of the firmament.[34]

We see that the third message begins with a reemphasis of the directive to pray the daily Rosary, but with the introduction of the title, "Our Lady of the Rosary". The goal of the recitation of the Rosary is again directed towards world peace and the end of the First World War, but it is accompanied by stating that it is through, and *only through*, the intercession of Mary that help can be obtained for world peace.

The third apparition also contains the vision of Hell, described by Lucia as a "sea of fire". In the fire were transparent human forms, both "souls and demons", with flames that issued from within themselves, who were shrieking in pain and despair. Lucia specified the appearance of the demons as resembling unknown but terrifying animals who were at once black and transparent. But in the midst of the agony of the vision and Mary's affirmation, Our Lady delivers a message of salvation. From the authority of the will of God (and not just her own), Mary speaks of the desire of God to establish the devotion to the Immaculate Heart of Mary as the divinely desired channel of salvation for sinners. The whole nature and purpose of Mary's role of salvific intercession takes its root in the will of God, and draws its legitimacy, its fittingness, and its call to faith and acceptance precisely in this providential grounding.

Mary then speaks of the result of responding to her requests: the salvation of numerous souls and peace. She predicts the close of the First World War, but is quick to predict the beginning of a worse war during the pontificate of Pope Pius XI,* if the world does not cease its outrages against God. One could find in this statement the implicit affirmation that war is a punishment for sin, a punishment called for in the order of justice for the increasing sin of humanity.[35] The effects of humanity's unwillingness to convert is foretold by Mary to consist of not only a second war, but also famine, persecutions of the Church, and specific sufferings for the Pope.

The theme of devotion to the Immaculate Heart is again called for, this time in the form of a consecration, and Eucharastic reparation is specified as an essential part of this devotion. Mary prophesied the effects if the requested devotion is not heeded, but affirms the final triumph of her Immaculate Heart in the end.[36] She then calls the children not to disclose what had been disclosed to them. It was not until 1942, at the request of her local bishop and a confirmation in prayer, that Sr. Lucia disclosed the first two parts of the three-part secret given to the children during the July 13 revelation, namely the vision of Hell and devotion to the Immaculate Heart of Mary.[37] The third part of the secret has yet to be disclosed to the public, but was given to Pope Pius XII and remains at present in the Vatican Archives.[38]

Fourth Apparition, August 13, 1917: The fourth Marian apparition does not offer significantly new content to the message development, but consists of some particular directives pertaining to the "festa" (a festival) for Our Lady of the Rosary, the building of a chapel (as was seen at Lourdes), along with a reaffirmation of the call to prayer and penance for sinners. The following is Lucia's account of the August 13 apparition:

---

* To the objection that the Second World War, 1939-1945, actually began during the pontificate of Pope Pius XII, Lucia has responded that the war in fact began with the occupation of Austria in 1938, which does fall under the reign of Pope Pius XI. The promised light that would illuminate the night as a sign of the forthcoming war does correspond with a reported aurora borealis that lit up the European skies on January 25, 1938. Cf. *Memoirs*, pp. 112, 187.

. . . Francisco and I saw the flash of light, which we called lightning. Jacinta arrived a moment later, we saw Our Lady on a holmoak tree.

"What do you want of me?"

"I want you to continue going to the Cova da Iria on the 13th, and to continue praying the Rosary every day. In the last month, I will perform a miracle so that all may believe."

"What do you want done with the money that the people leave in the Cova da Iria?"

"Have two litters made. One is to be carried by you and Jacinta and two other girls dressed in white; the other one is to be carried by Francisco and three other boys. The money from the litters is for the "festa" of Our Lady of the Rosary, and what is left over will help towards the construction of a chapel that is to be built here."

"I would like to ask you to cure some sick persons."

"Yes, I will cure some of them during the year."

Then, looking very sad, Our Lady said:

"Pray, pray, pray much, and make sacrifices for sinners; for many souls go to hell, because there are none to sacrifice themselves and to pray for them."

And she began to ascend as usual towards the east.[39]

Fifth Apparition, September 13, 1917: The message of the fifth apparition gives a further description of the sixth and final apparition, where Christ will appear, along with Mary's own final appearances as Our Lady of Dolours and Our Lady of Carmel, and the appearance of St. Joseph, greatest of all saints after Mary,[40] who will bless the world with the Child Jesus. The call to daily Rosary and a recognition of the efficacy of their penance as pleasing to God is also mentioned, as can be seen in Lucia's account of the fifth apparition:

At last we arrived at the Cova da Iria, and on reaching the holmoak we began to say the Rosary with the people. Shortly afterwards, we saw the flash of light, and then Our Lady appeared on the holmoak.

"Continue to pray the Rosary in order to obtain the end of the war. In October Our Lord will come, as well as Our Lady of Dolours and Our Lady of Carmel. Saint Joseph will appear with the Child Jesus to bless the world. God is pleased with your sacrifices. He does not want you to sleep with the rope on, but only to wear it during the day times."

"I was told to ask you many things, the cure of some sick people, of a deaf-mute. . . ."

"Yes, I will cure some, but not others. In October I will perform a miracle so that all may believe."

Then Our Lady began to rise as usual, and disappeared.[41]

Sixth Apparition, October 13, 1917: The final Marian apparition to Lucia, Jacinta, and Francisco in 1917 conveys a message that renews the overall message of Fatima: a call to prayer (particularly the Rosary), penance, conversion, peace, and an end to the ubiquitous offenses by humanity to its God. Lucia conveys the events of the sixth apparition as follows:

> . . . We reached the holmoak in the Cova da Iria. Once there, moved by an interior impulse, I asked the people to shut their umbrellas and say the Rosary. A little later, we saw the flash of light, and then Our Lady appeared on the holmoak.
>
> "What do you want of me?"
>
> "I want to tell you that a chapel is to be built here in my honour. I am the Lady of the Rosary. Continue always to pray the Rosary every day. The war is going to end, and the soldiers will soon return to their homes."
>
> "I have many things to ask you: the cure of some sick persons, the conversion of sinners and other things. . . ."
>
> "Some yes, but not others. They must amend their lives and ask forgiveness for their sins."
>
> Looking very sad, Our Lady said:
>
> "Do not offend the Lord our God any more, because He is already so much offended."
>
> Then, opening her hands, she made them reflect on the sun, and she ascended, the reflection of her own light continued to be projected on the sun itself. . . . After Our Lady had disappeared into the immense distance of the firmament, we beheld St. Joseph with the Child Jesus and Our Lady robed in white with a blue mantle, beside the sun. St. Joseph and the Child Jesus appeared to bless the world, for they traced the Sign of the Cross with their hands. When, a little later, this apparition disappeared, I saw Our Lord and Our Lady; it seemed to me that it was Our Lady of Dolours. Our Lord appeared to bless the world in the same manner as St. Joseph had done. This apparition also vanished, and I saw Our Lady once more, this time resembling Our Lady of Carmel.[42]

At the end of the appearances of this sixth apparition, the over seventy thousand on-lookers reported seeing what is known as the "solar miracle". Thousands of accounts have described the solar miracle as the sun appearing like a dull silver plate spinning around in a circular motion and described as dancing in the sky.[43] Seconds later, the sun was reported to have rushed downwards towards the earth, giving off various colors, and shortly before reaching the earth, it stopped in its course, and returned to its position in the sky.[44] Solar miracles, with a similar reference to the "spinning" and the "dancing" of the sun, have likewise been reported at Medjugorje.[45]

The message of the final Fatima apparition in 1917 accentuates the desire of Mary for an on-going, daily recitation of the Rosary, the need of conversion and repentence (in particular for those seeking the miraculous), and the directive for humanity to cease offending its Creator. The supernatural signs of the sixth apparition merely serve to affirm the call to prayer and penance in reparation to God and for the conversion of sinners achieved through devotion to the Immaculate Heart of Mary that comprises the general body of content revealed throughout the Fatima apparitions.

It was not until eight years later, on the evening of December 10, 1925, that Mary fulfilled her own prophecy from the first apparition on May 13, 1917 which foretold that she would return for a seventh time. Sister Lucia of the Immaculate Heart, in her convent at Pontevedia, Spain, received the seventh apparition of Mary which specified the directives mentioned in the third apparition of July 13, 1917, for the devotion to the Immaculate Heart of Mary, the consecration of Russia to the Immaculate Heart, and the First Saturday Communion of Reparation. Lucia gives the following account of the foretold seventh apparition (referring to herself in the third person):

> On December 10, 1925, the most Holy Virgin appeared to her, and by her side, elevated by a luminous cloud, was a child. The most Holy Virgin rested her hand on her shoulder, and as she did so, she showed her a heart encircled by thorns, which she was holding in her hand. At the same time, the Child said:
> "Have compassion on the Heart of your most Holy Mother, covered with thorns, with which ungrateful men pierce it at every moment, and there is no one to make an act of reparation to remove them."
> Then the Holy Virgin said:
> "Look, my daughter, at my Heart, surrounded with thorns with which ungrateful men pierce me at every moment by their blasphemies and ingratitude. You at least try to console me, and say that I promise to assist at the hour of death, with the graces necessary for salvation, all those who, on the first Saturday of five consecutive months, shall confess, receive Holy Communion, recite five decades of the Rosary, and keep me company for fifteen minutes while meditating on the fifteen mysteries of the Rosary, with the intention of making reparation to me.[46]

This seventh apparition conveys a message that at once attests to the efficacy of the intercession of Mary for the salvation of souls, and the need for humanity to also offer reparation to that person designated by the will of God to be the channel by which humanity comes to Christ. Just as Mary has played a singular role in the participation in the redemption of humanity through the infinite merits of her Son, so too does Mary share in the pain and sorrow experienced by Christ for the ongoing sins of a humanity who fails to realize that it is redeemed and invited to the heavenly banquet. Hence, it is again the intention of Christ (as seen by the words of the Christ Child in this 1925 apparition) that reparation is also to be made to that Heart that lies most close to the Heart of Christ, for the blasphemies and offenses that this Immaculate Heart has received through her role as the providentially ordained channel to Christ.

Hence, the message of the Blessed Virgin Mary at Fatima represents a continuation of the fundamental call to prayer and penance in atonement to God and for the conversion of sinners found in the 1858 message of the Blessed Virgin to St. Bernadette at Lourdes. But Fatima contains not only a continuation of the message of Lourdes, but also a considerable contribution in the form of new developments by which to implement the Marian insistence on prayer and penance, particularly in the establishment[47] of the devotion to the Immaculate Heart of Mary, the five Saturday Communions of Reparation, and the explicit global call to peace. Let us now examine how the content of the message of Medjugorje relates as both the continuation of the Lourdes and the Fatima message, and as a new development in the Marian-related call to prayer and penance.

Medjugorje: A Continuation
of Fatima and Lourdes

The message of Medjugorje attributed to the Blessed Virgin Mary by the seven Croatian youths presents a continuation of the fundamental Marian call of Lourdes which experienced a significant development in the Marian apparitions at Fatima. Since the message of Lourdes can be said to be contained, from the perspective of content, in the message of Fatima,* we will proceed to discuss the Fatima message in the light of the Medjugorje content to illustrate the strands of continuation and development present, to be followed by an analysis of the unique development found in the Medjugorjian message.

From the outset of the Fatima apparitions embodied in the 1916 Angelic apparitions, the consistency of the Fatima message with the content of the message of Medjugorje is evident. The first apparition of the Angel in 1916 to the Portuguese children begins with identifying himself as the "Angel of Peace". It is significant that Mary identifies herself as the "Queen of Peace" shortly after the beginning of the reported 1981 apparitions.[48] The Angel of Peace proceeds to call the children to pray a revealed prayer that includes the themes of faith in God, trust in God, and love of God, followed by prayer for unbelievers. This parallels the Medjugorjian calls to prayer, faith, conversion, abandonment to God, and adoration of the Incarnate God in the Eucharist.[49] The efficacy of devotion to the Hearts of Jesus and Mary is then stated by

* Since this chapter seeks to illustrate the continuity and "historical" development between the messages of Lourdes, Fatima, and Medjugorje, there will be no separate comparison of the messages of Lourdes and Medjugorje. But because of the incorporation of the Lourdes message to prayer and penance for reparation and conversion into the Fatima message, the message of Lourdes and the message of Medjugorje will nonetheless be implicitly compared.

the Angel. The same devotional call to the Hearts of Jesus and Mary is contained in the several requests of Mary at Medjugorje for daily consecrations to the Sacred and Immaculate Hearts.[50]

The second apparition of the Angel of Peace in 1916 begins with an emphatic call to ''Pray! Pray very much!'' resembling the numerous calls to ''Pray, pray, pray!''[51] found in the message of Medjugorje. The directive to continually offer sacrifices to God is also found in Mary's Thursday messages to the parish, asking them to endure their sufferings and to ''offer them as your sacrifice to God.''[52]

The Angel's request for prayer in reparation for the conversion of sinners, how God continues to be offended through the sins of humanity, the acceptance of providentially ordained suffering, and peace as the goal which is achievable only through conversion, all consistently correspond to the Medjugorjian themes of penance, conversion, offering of sufferings and sacrifices, abandonment to God, and the goal of peace.[53]

The third apparition from the Angel of Peace brings with it a message of Eucharistic adoration and reparation, and a petition for the conversion of sinners through the Hearts of Jesus and Mary. Likewise in the message of Medjugorje there is the explicit call to Eucharistic adoration, where Mary herself joins those in adoring the Christ indwelling,[54] the call to make reparation to the Almighty who is ''still suffering, because of your sins'',[55] Mary's directive to the parish to ''Pray these days for the conversion of sinners'',[56] and the call for daily consecration to the Hearts of Jesus and Mary as an instrument of deep conversion.[57]

The same essential consistency in message content between the Fatima messages and the message of Medjugorje continue in the 1917 Marian apparitions. The initial Marian apparition on May 13, 1917, consists, from a doctrinal and thematic viewpoint, in the attestation to the reality of Heaven and Purgatory, the efficacy of the Rosary (in reference to the requisites for Francisco's immediate entry into Heaven), the call for self-abandonment to God and the patient endurance of providential sufferings in reparation for the conversion of sinners, an example of Eucharistic adoration, and finally the call to daily Rosary as prayer for the goal of peace. The Medjugorjian message content certainly attests to the reality of Heaven and Purgatory, as the visionaries reported seeing both experiences of afterlife.[58] The call to daily Rosary and its efficacy for the conversion of sinners is evident in the message received by Jakov to ''let all the prayers which you say in your houses in the evening be said for the conversion of sinners. . . . Pray the Rosary every evening.''[59] The call to ''abandon yourselves totally to God''[60] in Mary's Thursday message to the parish coincides with the Fatima call of self-offering, and the thanks given for the ''offering of all your pains to God, even now when he is testing you''[61] corresponds with the Fatima request to willingly endure sufferings received from the Lord.

The message of Mary to the Portuguese shepherd children on June 13, 1917, begins with a renewed request for the daily Rosary, as is the case in the reported Medjugorjian message of August 14, 1984, calling for the daily recitation of the full fifteen decade Rosary.[62]

Our Lady of the Rosary proceeds to attest to the need of conversion and faith before the cure of a sick person is to take place, corresponding to the directive of the Queen of Peace in regard to the requested healing of Danijel Setku for the parents to first ''firmly believe''.[63] The desire of Mary to establish a world devotion to the Immaculate Heart is thematically consistent with the Medjugorjian call to consecration to the Immaculate Heart of Mary; and the salvific efficacy that arises from Mary's intercessory role in regard to devotion to the Immaculate Heart is also referred to in this Thursday message to the parish where Mary states that ''My son Jesus wishes to bestow on you special graces through me.''[64]

The third Marian apparition at Fatima on July 13, 1917 begins with the same renewed call to the daily Rosary in order to obtain peace for the world through Mary's intercession. Our Lady of the Rosary then promises a miracle as a sign to unbelievers to occur at the end of the apparitions, in a manner similar to Mary's reported promise at Medjugorje to establish a miraculous sign at the end of the apparitions for those who are still reluctant to believe.[65] The Fatima message again states the need of prayer to obtain graces for cures, parallelling the Medjugorjian message stating that prayer, fasting, and penance is the cure for ailments of both body and soul.[66] The third apparition message then reaffirms the need for sacrificing oneself for sinners, and reveals the Christological prayer, for the conversion of sinners, and in reparation to the Immaculate Heart of Mary. As we have seen, the themes of abandonment, offering of suffering and sacrifice, and conversion are clearly present in the Medjugorjian message. Although there has not as yet been an explicit request for reparation to the Immaculate Heart at Medjugorje, the theme of the suffering experienced by Mary because of the sinfulness of the world and the lack of global response to her Son is evident in the November 6, 1983 message transmitted by Jelena: ''Consider how sinful the world is today . . . how how many have tepid faith, and do not listen to Jesus. If you only knew what I go through, you would never sin again.''[67]

The third Marian apparition at Fatima continues with the vision of Hell, a vision also reportedly seen by some of the visionaries of Medjugorje.[68] Mary then tells the Portuguese children that it is by responding to her in devotion to the Immaculate Heart as the divinely ordained channel to salvation that will eventually lead them to peace, which is certainly the same goal posed by the Medjugorjian message.[69] This is followed by the eschatological prophecy of both world catastrophe (if her message is not heeded) and the ultimate victory of the Immaculate Heart in the world. The message of Medjugorje also speaks of the consequences of world catastrophe if the message of Mary is not accepted and lived, but for the believers to rest confident in the fact that in the midst of the world chastisement that awaits an unrepented world, divine peace should remain in the hearts of believers. This is almost as if to place the eschatological urgency always in the perspective of the gift of the peace of Christ that transcends the events of this world.[70] The request for the Five Saturdays of Eucharistic Reparation does not find an explicit counterpart in the Medjugorjian message, but certainly the theme of reparation in Mary's call to "make atonement for sins committed against the Sacred Heart"[71] and the theme of Eucharistic adoration and daily Mass are consistent with this specific Fatima directive. This is likewise the case with the specific Fatima call to consecrate Russia to Mary's Immaculate Heart, but the statement of Medjugorje that it will be in Russia that God will eventually be most glorified[72] may correspond to both the fulfillment of the desired consecration of Russia and the eventual triumph of the Immaculate Heart prophesied at Fatima.

The fourth Marian apparition on August 13, 1917 began with the affirmation of the need to continue the daily Rosary and that the promised sign at the end of the apparitions was to happen. There is also the prediction of cures to take place during the year. A number of cures have already been reported to follow prayer and fasting as directed by the message of Medjugorje.[73] Our Lady of the Rosary then makes an emphatic call for continued prayer and sacrifices for sinners. "Pray, pray, pray very much, and make sacrifices for sinners; many souls go to Hell, because there are none to sacrifice themselves and pray for them."[74] This Fatima message has a strong correlation with the Medjugorjian message to "Pray these days for the conversion of sinners. . . . Because the world is in great sin"[75] and the message Mary conveyed while showing some of the visionaries Purgatory: "Those people are waiting for your prayers and sacrifices."[76]

The September 13, 1917 apparition of Mary at Fatima primarily consists of the description of the sixth apparition, along with the ever-present reminder to recite the daily Rosary. The fifth apparition also contains a word of thanks for the sacrifices offered, describing them as penitential acts pleasing to God. Besides the clear call to penance in the message of Medjugorje,[77] Mary's words of thanks at Fatima resemble this 1984 Thursday message to the parish of St. James: "Dear children! Today I am very happy because there are many of those who desire to devote themselves to me. I thank you! My Son Jesus Christ wishes to bestow upon you special graces through me. My Son is happy because of your dedication. Thank you because you have responded to my call."[78] Mary has also specified the nature of the penance to be performed,[79] as is likewise visible in the Fatima specification to the children not to wear the penitential robe to bed.

The sixth apparition to Lucia, Jacinta, and Francisco on October 13, 1917, identifies Mary as the "Lady of the Rosary", whereas after Mary's initial self-identification as "the Virgin Mary", she called herself the "Queen of Peace". The same change in title can be seen between Fatima and Lourdes, where Mary stated she was the "Immaculate Conception". Mary then reemphasizes the imperative of the daily Rosary for the final time, as she has reportedly done numerous time at Medjugorje,[80] states the need for repentance and conversion as a prerequisite for the miraculous, which is also present in the Medjugorjian message,[81] and calls for an end to the offenses against the Lord who is already much offended. The same call to conversion and reparation is present in the message of Medjugorje, accentuated in this 1984 Lenten message at Medjugorje to "make an atonement for the wounds inflicted in the Heart of my Son . . . offended by all sorts of sins."[82] It is also interesting to note that visions of Mary with the Child Jesus, of Mary in the presence of angels, and numerous accounts of solar miracles have likewise been reported at Medjugorje.[83]

The seventh apparition of the Blessed Virgin Mary to Sr. Lucia on December 10, 1925, begins by calling for "compassion on the Heart of your most Holy Mother", referring to the call to reparation to the Immaculate Heart. The transmitted message of April 14, 1984, "Dear children! Sympathize with me. Pray, pray, pray,"[84] seems to plea for the same type of compassion that will bear fruit in a ceasing of the numerous sins by which the Immaculate Heart is pierced. The specifications of the five first Saturdays of reparation does not appear in the Medjugorjian content, but the individual directives to monthly Confession,[85] daily Mass and the reception of the Eucharist,[86] and the daily recitation and meditation of the fifteen decades in the Rosary[87] are explicit developmental themes in the Medjugorjian content. The intention of performing these acts out of reparation to the Immaculate Heart is not an explicit directive in the message of Medjugorje, but an attestation to the suffering experienced by Mary through a lack of prayer and penance does have its grounding in the message, as was previously mentioned.

It is therefore evident that the basic doctrinal and thematic elements originally found in the message of the Blessed Virgin Mary at Lourdes, and its fundamental development perceivable in the message of Mary at Fatima is also found to be present in the messages reported by the seven Croatian visionaries at Medjugorje, but accompanied with an even greater development of the basic Marian call to prayer and penance in reparation to God and for the conversion of sinners. This is not to suggest that every detail revealed in the message of Fatima can be explicitly located in the Medjugorjian message.[88] But it is to state that every theme manifested in the Fatima apparition has an explicit doctrinal and thematic continuation in the message of Medjugorje—a consistency of content that shows a development, but without any essential change in direction, much less any contradiction in content.

Medjugorje: New Elements in the Marian Message

The development between the message of Lourdes and the message of Fatima certainly admits of new elements besides the doctrinal and thematic consistency that bridges the two apparitions (for example the focus on the Hearts of Jesus and Mary and the call for first Saturday Communions of Reparation). The same introduction of new elements, but while remaining doctrinally and thematically consistent with the previous Marian messages at Lourdes and Fatima, is seen in the message of Medjugorje. It is important to recognize that these new elements do not change the essential direction of Marian development begun at Lourdes, but does offer new modes by which to implement the rudimentary call to prayer and penance for reparation to God and conversion of sinners.

It is worthy to note that of the six foundational themes present in the message of Medjugorje (namely faith, prayer, fasting, penance, conversion, and peace) the only new element not explicitly contained in the message of Fatima is the call to fasting. And yet, the doctrinal and thematic consistency between the Fatima and Medjugorje message is obvious, since fasting comprises a specific means of the general call to penance. The introduction of fasting also points to the legitimate development found in the Medjugorjian message by way of a new specification for implementing the same fundamental Marian call.*

The new elements of the message of Medjugorje that do appear in the Fatima message, as found in the developmental themes, are the following: Renewal in the Holy Spirit, Renewal of Sacred Scripture, Ecumenism, and the emphasis on Family and Community Prayer. And yet, these identical four themes have been grouped together and designated as new elements in another strand of development—namely, as an aspect of the principal emphases to arise out of the development promulgated in Vatican Council II and the post-conciliar teaching and guidance of the

---

* It is also worthy to note that in 1917 the practice of fasting was a determinate aspect of the Church-directed norms for Christian asceticism to which every Catholic was obliged, whereas fasting in the Church today can be substituted by a variety of other penances. Cf. Paul VI, *Apostolic Constitution in Fasting and Abstinence*.

Magisterium. Not only have we seen that the call to Renewal in the Holy Spirit, Renewal in Sacred Scripture, Ecumenism, and Family and Community Prayer, are all firmly grounded in the conciliar and post-conciliar teachings of the Magisterium,[89] but these four aspects of the Christian life have also experienced a particular renewal in the post-conciliar life of the Church, which have received the support and encouragement of the Magisterium.[90] For example, the endorsement of the Magisterium of authentic forms of contemporary movements such as the Charismatic Renewal,[91] scripture study groups,[92] ecumenical conferences,[93] and *Communione e Liberazione* (an Italian-based organization fostering youth community prayer)[94] attest to the Magisterium's encouragement of these post-conciliar themes, not merely because of their appearance in the post-conciliar life of the Church, but because of their welcomed appearance as magisterially sound developments in the efforts of the Church to direct its members to prayer, asceticism, and peace, leading them to Christian perfection.[95]

Summary Statement

We can thereby end this comparison of the message of Medjugorje with the messages of Lourdes and Fatima with the following conclusions. Firstly, that the message of Medjugorje contains all the fundamental Marian themes present in the message of Lourdes and the message of Fatima, the nature of which can be summarized in the call of Mary for prayer and penance performed in reparation to God (and secondarily to Mary herself) for the sins of humanity, in supplication for the conversion of sinners, and for peace for the entire human family.

Secondly, the message of Medjugorje offers a development in the Marian call to prayer, penance, and peace by way of specification in the manner by which humanity is to implement these fundamental calls (e.g. the call to fasting as a new means by which to implement the more general call to penance).

Thirdly, the message of Medjugorje offers new elements not previously seen in the message of Fatima and Lourdes. But these new elements are in no sense contrary to the fundamental Marian call to prayer and penance, but instead comprise new means by which to implement the same Marian call—means that are recognizably and authentically post-conciliar.*

* Apart from the particular authenticity of the reported apparitions at Medjugorje, it would seem fitting that the message transmitted by Mary at any given period of Church history would reflect the same degree of development as manifested by the Church's Magisterium during the same historical period, since both Mary and the Church's Magisterium remain under the Holy Spirit: one in the singularity of truth by which He guides, and one in the degree of development He sees as appropriate for the Church in any given historical period.

Notes
Chapter Five

[1] Alan Heame, *The Happenings at Lourdes*, London, Catholic Book Club, 1968, p. 71. Note: This text has been chosen as the primary source for this section due to its dependence on the French definitive work, R. Laurentin, Lourdes, *Documents Authentiques*, 6 Vols., P. Lethilleux, 1957.

[2] *Ibid.*, p. 76.

[3] *Ibid.*, p. 78.

[4] J. B. Estrade, J. H. Girolestone, tr., *The Appearance of the Blessed Virgin Mary at the Grotto of Lourdes*, Art and Book Co., Ltd., Westminister, 1912, p. 51.

[5] Heame, *Lourdes*, p. 80.

[6] Estrade, *Appearances*, pp. 56-57.

[7] Heame, *Lourdes*, p. 82.

[8] Estrade, *Appearances*, p. 79.

[9] Heame, *Lourdes*, p. 84.

[10] *Ibid.*

[11] Estrade, *Appearances*, p. 84.

[12] Heame, *Lourdes*, p. 85.

[13] Estrade, *Appearances*, p. 89.

[14] *Ibid.*, p. 94.

[15] Heame, *Lourdes*, p. 90.

[16] *Ibid.*, p. 91.

[17] *Ibid.*, p. 92.

[18] *Ibid.*, p. 93.

[19] Estrade, *Appearances*, p. 114.

[20] *Ibid.*

[21] *Ibid.*, pp. 122-123.

[22] *Ibid.*, p. 127.

[23] *Ibid.*, pp. 130-131.

[24] Rev. Robert Fox, *Fatima Today*, Virginia, Christendom Publications, 1983, p. 14.

[25] Lucia is referring to the same Angel that appeared to her and three other companions briefly in 1915. Cf. *Fatima in Lucia's Own Words*, Second Memoir, p. 60.

[26] Louis Kondor, S.V.D., ed., *Fatima in Lucia's Own Words: Sister Lucia's Memoirs*, Postulation Centre, Fatima, Portugal, distributed by Our Blessed Lady of Victory Mission, Inc., Brookings, South Dakota, 1976, Second Memoir, p. 62.

[27] *Ibid.*

[28] Jacinta and Francisco had not yet received their first communion, but evidently neither regarded this as a sacramental communion. Cf. *Memoirs*, footnote 18, p. 99.

[29] *Ibid.*, p. 63.

[30] *Ibid.*, Fourth Memoir, p. 160.

[31] This last line was omitted in Lucia's final account of the 1917 apparitions, but appears in other earlier accounts as it is cited in this text. Cf. *Memoirs*, p. 187, Footnote 14.

[32] *Ibid.*, Fourth Memoir, p. 161.

[33] *Memoirs and Letters of Sr. Lucia*, p. 409, as it appears in Joseph Pelletier, A.A., *Exciting Fatima News: Recently Revealed in Sister Lucy's Letters*, Assumption Publication, Massachusetts, 1975, p. 46.

[34] *Memoirs*, Fourth Memoir, pp. 162-166.

[35] Cf. St. Thomas Aquinas, *De Malo*, Q. 1-2.

[36] For a more complete treatment of the call to a consecration of Russia to the Immaculate Heart of Mary and the First Saturday Communions of Reparation, see J. Haffert, *Russia Will Be Converted*, AMI Press, New Jersey, 1950, and J. Pelletier, A.A., *Exciting Fatima News*, Assumption Publication, Massachusetts, 1975.

[37] *Memoirs*, Third Memoir, p. 101.

[38] *Ibid.*, p. 113.

[39] *Ibid.*, Fourth Memoir, pp. 166-167.

[40] Cf. G. Garrigou-La Grange, O.P., *Mother of the Saviour and Our Interior Life*, Appendix I, St. Louis, Herder, 1949.

[41] *Memoirs*, Fourth Memoir, p. 168.

[42] *Ibid.*, pp. 169-170.

[43] F. Johnston, *Fatima: The Great Sign*, Augustine Publishing, Devon, p. 53 ff.

[44] *Ibid.*

[45] Cf. Rooney, *Mary, Queen of Peace*, p. 80. Cf. *supra*, Chapter I, section 3.

[46] *Memoirs*, Fourth Memoir, p. 168.

[47] By stating that Mary "established" devotion to the Immaculate Heart is not to suggest that devotion to the heart of Mary did not exist as a devotional practice in the Church before the Fatima apparitions, as is evident particularly in the writings of St. John Eudes. Cf. J. Aumann, O.P., *History of Spirituality*, p. 253.

[48] Cf. *supra*, Chapter II, Foundational Themes (hereafter "FT"), section 6.

[49] Cf. *supra*, Chapter II, FT, sections 1, 2, 3, 5, and Developmental Themes (hereafter "DT"), sections 4, 13.

[50] Cf. *supra*, Chapter II, DT, section 8.

[51] Cf. *supra*, Chapter II, FT, section 2.

[52] Cf. *supra*, Chapter II, DT, section 12.

[53] Cf. *supra*, Chapter II, FT, sections 4, 5, 6; DT, sections 12, 13.

[54] Cf. *supra*, Chapter II, DT, section 4.

[55] Cf. *supra*, Chapter II, DT, section 12.

[56] Cf. *supra*, Chapter II, FT, section 5.

[57] Cf. *supra*, Chapter II, DT, section 8.

[58] Cf. *supra*, Chapter II, DT, section 9.

[59] Cf. *supra*, Chapter I, section 7.

[60] Cf. *supra*, Chapter II, DT, section 13.

[61] Cf. *supra*, Chapter II, DT, section 12.

[62] Cf. *supra*, Chapter I, section 7.

[63] Cf. *supra*, Chapter I, section 2.

[64] Cf. *supra*, Chapter II, DT, section 3.

[65] Cf. *supra*, Chapter I, sections 1 and 2.

[66] Cf. *supra*, Chapter I, section 3.

[67] Cf. *supra*, Chapter I, section 6.

[68] Cf. *supra*, Chapter II, DT, section 9.

[69] Cf. *supra*, Chapter II, FT, section 6.

[70] Cf. *supra*, Chapter I, section 6.

[71] Cf. *supra*, Chapter I, section 7.

[72] Cf. *supra*, Chapter I, section 3.

[73] Cf. R. Laurentin, *Is the Virgin Mary Appearing at Medjugorje?*, Appendix 4, p. 150.

[74] *Memoirs*, Fourth Memoir, p. 167.

[75] Cf. *supra*, Chapter II, FT, section 5.

[76] Cf. *supra*, Chapter I, section 3.

[77] Cf. *supra*, Chapter II, FT, section 4.

[78] Cf. *supra*, Chapter I, section 7.

[79] Cf. *supra*, Chapter I, section 6.

[80] Cf. *supra*, Chapter II, DT, section 6.

[81] Cf. *supra*, Chapter I, section 1.

[82] Cf. *supra*, Chapter II, DT, section 8.

[83] Svetozar Kraljevic, O.F.M., *Appearances of Our Lady of Medjugorje*, original manuscript, p. 23; L. Rooney, *Mary, Queen of Peace*, p. 80.

[84] Cf. *supra*, Chapter II, FT, section 2.

[85] Cf. *supra*, Chapter II, DT, section 5.

[86] Cf. *supra*, Chapter II, DT, section 4.

[87] Cf. *supra*, Chapter II, DT, section 6.

[88] This also holds true between the messages of Lourdes and Fatima (e.g., the explicit call to "penance" that appears in the message of Lourdes is not seen in the message of Fatima).

[89] Cf. *supra*, Chapter IV, sections 2, 7, 10, and 11.

[90] Fr. Gerald McGinnity, *Medjugorje*, original manuscript, Rome, Irish Pontifical College, 1984.

[91] Cf. Paul VI, Address to National Conference of Charismatic Renewal, May 19, 1975, A.A.S. (67), 1975.

[92] Cf. *supra*, Chapter IV, section 7.

[93] For example, the Twentieth Anniversary Conference of *Nostrae Aetate* in 1985, held at the Pontifical University of St. Thomas Aquinas and attended by Cardinal Wildebrands, Vatican secretary for ecumenism.

[94] Pope John Paul II has manifested support for *Comunione e Liberazione* by his frequent meetings with the organizations in Rome at his summer residence, Castel Gandolfo.

[95] Flannery, *Vatican II, Lumen Gentium*, Chapter V, p. 396.

CONCLUSION

The message of Medjugorje, that body of individual messages reported by seven Croatian youths in the mountain village of Medjugorje, Yugoslavia, and attributed to the Blessed Virgin Mary during almost daily apparitions that began on June 24, 1981, and continue to present (March, 1985), has been the focus of this examination.

In examining the foundational themes of the message of Medjugorje and comparing them to the Gospel of Jesus Christ and to the writings of the Apostolic Fathers, we found the presence of all six foundational themes clearly grounded in these two sources of Christian truth. That the themes of faith, prayer, fasting, penance, conversion, and peace echo the words of Christ in Sacred Scripture is a clear attestation to the doctrinal soundness of these six Medjugorjian themes. The evidence of the same six themes in the writings of the Apostolic Fathers illustrates that these six calls to Christian prayer and asceticism comprised an essential element of the Christian life in the earliest assembly of the infant Church in her efforts to be true to Christ and the Apostles. Hence, the heart of the message of Medjugorje possesses a doctrinal consistency with the heart of the Christian message in its earliest and least developed formulation.

The fourteen developmental themes that arise from the message of Medjugorje were then examined in the light of the most contemporary development of authentic Catholic truth, namely the Documents of Vatican Council II and post-conciliar documents as promulgated by the Church's Magisterium. This examination led to the conclusion that all fourteen developmental themes were rooted in the official teaching of the Magisterium, which illustrates the contemporary, post-conciliar, and doctrinally orthodox nature of the developmental aspect of the message of Medjugorje.

Finally, after comparing the message of Medjugorje to the messages revealed at the ecclesiastically approved apparitions of the Blessed Virgin Mary at Lourdes, France in 1858, and at Fatima, Portugal in 1917, the message of Medjugorje was found to contain all the principal doctrinal themes present in the messages of Fatima and Lourdes. Further, the message of Medjugorje seems to embody not only the fundamental Marian call to prayer and penance contained in the Fatima and Lourdes messages, but also a significant development in the Marian message by way of specification as to the means for implementing the continuing Marian call (in much the same fashion as can be seen in the legitimate development between the message of Lourdes and the message of Fatima). Furthermore, the Medjugorjian message offers new elements in the Marian call to prayer and penance, and for conversion, all of which are clearly and authentically post-conciliar in nature.

Hence, an analysis of the content of the message of Medjugorje leads one to conclude that regardless of the question of the authenticity of the reported Marian apparitions in Medjugorje, the calls contained in the message of Medjugorje represent an authentic embodiment of Catholic doctrine that is grounded in the divinely revealed source of the Gospel of Jesus Christ, and the contemporary formulation of divine revelation in the teachings of the Church's Magisterium. Based on this fact, and this fact alone, the calls to Christian prayer, asceticism, and a full living of the Christian life in general contained in the message of Medjugorje oblige all Christians to their faithful observance, as directives divinely revealed by the Father, through the Son, and in the Holy Spirit.

I would like to end this examination of the message of Medjugorje, a message that ultimately points to the peace of Christ offered to the modern world through Mary, Queen of Peace, by the following excerpt from the writings of Fr. Reginald Garrigou-La Grange, O.P., a world-renowned theologian during the middle decades of this century, who in a type of theological prophecy, synthesizes the goal of the Medjugorjian message:

> Exterior peace will not be obtained for the world except by the interior peace of souls, bringing them back to God and working to establish the reign of Christ in the depths of their intellects, of their hearts, and of their wills. For this return of straying souls to Him Who alone can save them, it is necessary to have recourse to the intercession of Mary, Universal Mediatrix and Mother of all men. It is said of sinners who seem forever lost that they must be confided to Mary: it is the same for Christian peoples who stray. All the influence of the Blessed Virgin has its end to lead them to Her Son. . . .
>
> That is why on all sides many interior souls, before the unprecedented disorders and tragic sufferings of the hour, feel the need for recourse to the redeeming love of Christ through the intercession of Mary Mediatrix.*

---

* Reginald Garrigou-La Grange, O.P., *The Mother of the Saviour and Our Interior Life*, translated by Bernard Kelly, C.S.S.P., Dublin, Golden Books, Ltd., 1948, p. 317.

APPENDIX I

Revealed Prayers from Fatima and Medjugorje

The following prayers were revealed at the Marian apparitions at Fatima and at the reported apparitions at Medjugorje. The prayers from Fatima are taken from St. Lucia's memoirs, and the Medjugorjian prayers have been translated from the Italian into English. (Note: Bracketed words represent added words present in the common usage of these prayers).

Revealed Prayers at Fatima

Prayer of Reparation: Given by the Angel of Peace at the first 1916 apparition.

> My God, I believe, I adore, I hope, and I love you! [And] I ask [pardon] for those who do not believe, do not adore, do not hope and do not love you.

According to the directions of the Angel, this prayer is to be said three times while kneeling with one's head bowed down until the forehead touches the ground.

Prayer of Eucharistic Offering and Reparation: Given by the Angel of Peace at the third apparition of 1916.

> Most Holy Trinity, Father, Son and Holy Spirit, I offer you the most precious Body, Blood, Soul, and Divinity of Jesus Christ, present in all the tabernacles of the world, in reparation for the outrages, sacrileges, and indifference with which He Himself is offended. And, through the infinite merits of His most Sacred Heart and the Immaculate Heart of Mary, I beg of You the conversion of poor sinners.

Aspiration to the Trinity and the Blessed Sacrament: Said by the children through an inspired interior impulse during the first apparition of the Blessed Virgin on May 13, 1917.

> O most Holy Trinity, I adore you! My God, my God, I love you in the most Blessed Sacrament.

Rosary Prayer of Reparation: To be said at the end of each mystery of the Rosary, as revealed during the third Marian apparition of July 13, 1917.

O my Jesus, forgive us [our sins]; save us from the fires of hell; lead all souls to Heaven, especially those who are in most need [of Your mercy].

Revealed Prayers at Medjugorje

Prayer of Consecration to the Immaculate Heart of Mary: On April 19, 1983, Jelena Vasilj asked Mary how to consecrate oneself to her Immaculate Heart. Jelena reported receiving the following prayer of consecration (obtained from St. James Parish, Medjugorje).

O my Mother,
Mother of goodness, of love and mercy,
I love you infinitely,
and I offer myself to you.

Through your goodness, your love
and your grace, save me.
I love you infinitely,
and I desire that you protect me.

From the bottom of my heart I pray to you,
Mother of goodness,
give me your goodness.
Give it so that I may gain Heaven through it.
I pray to you, for your infinite love,
to give me the graces
so that I may love each man,
as you loved Jesus Christ.

I pray that you may give me the grace
to be "merciful toward you".*
I offer myself totally to you and I desire
that you watch over my every step.

---

* The prayer was distributed with the following footnote attached to it in reference to the noted verse in the fourth stanza. Some theologians and priests have immediately stumbled on this verse and said: "How can a girl forgive the Blessed Mother?" "What has she to forgive the Blessed Mother for?" Others have immediately realized the profundity of the prayer, and they have recognized in the verse a part of spiritual life which is hidden from many Christians—the "pardonability to God".

The seer explains the verse as follows: "The Blessed Mother told me several times: 'Excuse me, but I can't give it to you, because it's not according to God's will.' Therefore the phrase 'I pray that you may give me the grace to be merciful towards you' means: 'Give me the grace of loving your will which is different from mine.' "

Because you are full of grace,
and I want to never forget this.
And if I should ever lose my graces,
I pray that you will restore them back to me.

Amen.

Prayer of Consecration to the Sacred Heart of Jesus: This prayer of
consecration to the Sacred Heart of Jesus was reportedly dictated by the
Blessed Virgin Mary to Jelena Vasilj on November 28, 1983. It is
followed by a second prayer of consecration to the Immaculate Heart of
Mary, received on the same day.

O Jesus, we know that you have been gentle
and that you have offered your Heart for us.
It is crowned with thorns and with our sins.
We know that you pray every day
so that we may not be lost.

Jesus, remember us when we fall into sin.
Through your most holy Heart
make all people love one another.

Dispel hatred between men,
Show us your love.
We all love you,
and desire that you protect us
with Your Shepherd's Heart
from every sin.

Enter into every heart, Jesus!
Knock, knock at the door of our heart.
Be patient and persevering.
We are still closed because
we have not understood Your will.

Knock continually!

O good Jesus, make us
open our hearts to You,
at least in the moment when
we remember Your passion,
suffered for us.

Amen.

Prayer of Consecration to the Immaculate Heart of Mary: November
28, 1983.

O Immaculate Heart of Mary, full of goodness,
show Your love towards us.

That the flames of Your Heart, O Mary
may descend upon all humanity.

We love You indefinitely.
Imprint on our hearts true love
so that we may have everlasting
desire for You.

O Mary, gentle and humble of heart,
remember us when we are in sin.
You know that all man sins.
Grant to us, through Your Immaculate and
Maternal Heart, to be protected from every
spiritual sickness.

Make us always look
to the goodness of Your Motherly Heart;
and convert us through the flame
of Your Heart.

Amen.

The Rosary of Jesus Christ: The Rosary of Jesus Christ is a seven-point meditation on the life of Jesus, intermingled with other prayers and songs. Although a form of this Rosary had been previously used by the Croatian Franciscans, this specific adoption was reportedly revealed by Mary through Jelena Vasilj, to be used by the youth prayer group at Medjugorje.

Begin with the recitation of the *Creed*.

Meditation 1—How was Jesus born? In a cave of shepherds far from home, in extreme poverty. He turned to the humble before everyone else. He gave Himself above all to Mary and Joseph. How can Jesus be born *in me*? With my full conversion to Him. He finds in me the same poverty of Bethlehem, but if I open myself to Him, He makes me rich in Him. How can we make Him to be born *in others*? By praying, fasting, witnessing with our actions. . . .

Pause for meditation: a) five *Our Fathers*, slowly and with concentration; b) to be said with Mary, *O God, be my strength and protection*; c) an appropriate song (or a prayer to Mary).

Meditation 2—How Jesus loved the poor, the weak, the outcast, the weary, the sick, the sinner. How shall *I* love them? Whom shall I prefer? How can I help them? How can I make amends for sinners? How can I help *others* to love, in the example of Jesus?

Pause for meditation: a) five *Our Fathers*, slowly and with concentration; b) to be said with Mary, *O God, be my strength and protection*; c) an appropriate song (or a prayer to Mary).

Meditation 3—How Jesus has been totally opened to God, outstretched to do His will. How shall *I* open myself to God with full availability to His will, even when it costs, convinced that it is for my greatest good? How can I help *others to open themselves*, to understand the gift of God's will?

Pause for meditation: a) five *Our Fathers*, slowly and with concentration; b) to be said with Mary, *O God, be my strength and protection*; c) an appropriate song (or a prayer to Mary).

Meditation 4—How Jesus infinitely trusted His Father, even in the difficult moments. How shall *I* abandon myself in faith, and remove every fear from my heart? How can I reassure *others*, to spread trust and security in God's providence?

Pause for meditation: a) five *Our Fathers*, slowly and with concentration; b) to be said with Mary, *O God, be my strength and protection*; c) an appropriate song (or a prayer to Mary).

Meditation 5—How Jesus was willing not only to listen to God, but also *to give Himself to death on the cross*. How shall I give *myself* to God until the end of my life out of love? How can I help *others* to give themselves totally to God, above all when they are called to the consecrated life?

Pause for meditation: a) five *Our Fathers*, slowly and with concentration; b) to be said with Mary, *O God, be my strength and protection*; c) an appropriate song (or a prayer to Mary).

Meditation 6—How Jesus has conquered death, and has given to the Apostles the experience of the resurrection. How shall *I myself* rise from evil, experience the joy of resurrection, communicate it? How can I bring *others* to the joy of resurrection, to the hope of Heaven?

Pause for meditation: a) five *Our Fathers*, slowly and with concentration; b) to be said with Mary, *O God, be my strength and protection*; c) an appropriate song (or a prayer to Mary).

Meditation 7—How Jesus has risen to Heaven and sent the Holy Spirit to the Apostles. How shall I too rise spiritually, with the grace of the Holy Spirit, reviving the hope of Heaven? How can I help *others* to progress spiritually, calling upon them the Holy Spirit?

Pause for meditation: a) five *Our Fathers*, slowly and with concentration; b) to be said with Mary, *O God, be my strength and protection*; c) an appropriate song (or a prayer to Mary).

Conclude by reciting seven *Glory be's*.

APPENDIX II

Medjugorjian Message Update

The following messages contribute the most recently reported messages from the visionaries, and includes some information concerning the visionaries themselves in regards to their role as conveyors of the Medjugorjian message. The messages will be listed according to the message categories cited in Chapter I.

Thursday Messages to the Parish, March 14 to October 24, 1985

March 14, 1985: "Dear children! In your life you have all experienced light and darkness. God gives to each person knowledge of good and evil. I am calling you to the light, which you have to carry to all people who are in darkness. From day to day, people who are in darkness come to your homes. Give them, dear children, the light. Thank you for your response to my call."

March 21, 1985: "Dear children! I want to give you the message and therefore, today also, I call you to live and to accept my messages. Dear children, I love you and in a special way I have chosen this parish, which is more dear to me than others where I have gladly been when the Almighty sent me. There I call to you: accept me, dear children, for your well being. Follow the messages. Thank you for your response to my call."

March 24, 1985 (Eve of the Annunciation): "Dear children! Today I wish to call you to Confession, even if you had Confession a few days ago. I wish you to experience my Feast Day within yourselves. You cannot, unless you give yourselves to God completely. And so I am calling you to reconciliation with God! Thank you for your response to my call."

March 29, 1985: "Dear children! Today I want to call you—pray, pray, pray! In prayer you will come to know the greatest joy and the way out of every situation that has no way out. Thank you for moving ahead in prayer. Every individual is dear to my heart. And I thank all of you who have rekindled prayer in your families. Thank you for your response to my call.''

April 4, 1985 (Holy Thursday): ''Dear children! I thank you because you begin to think of the glory of God in your hearts. Today is the day when I wished to stop giving the messages because some individuals did not accept me. The parish has responded, and I wish to continue giving you the messages, like never before in the history since the beginning of time. Thank you for your response to my call.''

April 5, 1985 (Good Friday): ''You, the parishioners, have a great and heavy cross. But do not be afraid to carry it. My Son is with you and He will help you.''

April 11, 1985: ''Dear children! Today I wish to say to everyone in the parish to pray in a special way for the enlightenment of the Holy Spirit. From today God wants to try the parish in a special way, in order that He might strengthen it in faith. Thank you for your response to my call.''

April 18, 1985: ''Dear children! Today I thank you for every opening of your hearts. Joy overwhelms me for every heart that opens to God, especially in the parish. Rejoice with me. Pray all the prayers for opening the sinful hearts. I want this. God wants this through me. Thank you for your response to my call.''

April 25, 1985: ''Dear children! Today I want to tell you to begin work in your hearts as you work in the fields. Work and change your hearts so that the spirit of God moves into the heart. Thank you for your response to my call.''

May 2, 1985: ''Dear children! Today I invite you to prayer in the hearts and not only by habit. Some are coming but do not move in prayer. Therefore I beg you as a Mother, pray that prayer prevails in your heart in every moment. Thank you for your response to my call.''

May 9, 1985: ''Dear children! You do not know how many graces God is giving you. These days when the Holy Spirit is working in a special way, you do not want to advance, your hearts are turned towards earthly things, and you are occupied by them. Turn your hearts to prayer and ask that the Holy Spirit be poured upon you. Thank you for your response to my call.''

May 16, 1985: ''Dear children! I am calling you to more attentive prayer, and more participation in the Mass. I wish you to experience God within yourselves during Mass. I wish to say to the youth, especially, be open to the Holy Spirit, because God wants to draw you to Himself these days when Satan is active. Thank you for your response to my call.''

May 23, 1985: ''Dear children! Open your hearts to the Holy Spirit in a special way these days. The Holy Spirit is working in a special way through you. Open your hearts and give your lives to Jesus, so that He works through your hearts and strengthens you. Thank you for your response to my call."

May 30, 1985: "I am calling you again to prayer of the heart. Let prayer, dear children, be your everyday food. In a special way now when work in the fields is exhausting you, you cannot pray with your heart. Pray and then you will overcome every tiredness. Prayer will be your happiness and rest. Thank you for your response to my call."

June 6, 1985: "Dear children! In these days many people of all nationalities will come to the parish, and now I am telling you to love. Love first of all members of your own family and then you might be able to accept in love all those who are coming. Thank you for your response to my call."

June 13, 1985: "Dear children! Until the anniversary day [June 25] I am calling you, you in the parish, to pray more, and let your prayer be a sign of your surrender to God. Dear children, I know about your tiredness. But you don't know how to surrender yourselves to me. These days, surrender yourselves to me completely. Thank you for your response to my call."

June 20, 1985: "Dear children! I wish for you this feast day [June 25] to open your hearts to the Lord of all hearts. Give me all your feelings and all your problems. I wish to console you in all your temptations. I wish to fill you with the peace, joy, and love of God. Thank you for your response to my call."

June 25, 1985: "Dear children! I ask you to ask everyone to pray the Rosary. With the Rosary you will overcome all the troubles which Satan is trying to inflict on the Catholic Church." Our Lady gave this message to Marija when she asked, "Madonna, what do you wish to say to priests?" "Let all priests pray the Rosary. Give time to the Rosary."

June 28, 1985: "Dear children! Today I give you the message through which I am calling you to humility. These days you have felt great joy because of all the people who were coming, and you have spoken about your experiences with love. Now I call you to continue in humility and with an open heart to speak to all those who are coming. Thank you for your response to my call."

July 4, 1985: "Dear children! Thank you for every sacrifice you have offered. And know I urge you to offer every sacrifice with love. I desire that you are helpless, and begin helping with trust, and the Lord will give to you always with trust. Thank you for your response to my call."

July 11, 1985: "Dear children! I love this parish and I protect it with my mantle from every work of Satan. Pray that Satan flees from the parish and from every individual that comes to this parish. In this way you will be able to hear every call and answer it with your life. Thank you for your response to my call.''

July 18, 1985: ''Dear children! Today I beg you to put more blessed objects in your homes, and that everyone carry blessed objects. Let everything be blessed so that Satan will tempt you less because you are armed against him. Thank you for your response to my call.''

July 25, 1985: ''Dear children! I want to shepherd you but you do not want to obey my messages. Today I call you to obey my messages. Then you will be able to live everything that God tells me to tell you. Open yourselves to God and God will work through you and give you everything you need. Thank you for your response to my call.''

August 1, 1985: ''Dear children! I want to tell you that I have chosen this parish. I protect it, holding it in my hands like a fragile little flower that struggles for life. I beg you to give yourselves to me so that I can offer you clean and without sin as a gift to God. Satan has taken one part of the plan, and he wants to have it all. Pray that he does not succeed, because I desire to have you for myself to offer you to God. Thank you for your response to my call.''

August 8, 1985: ''Dear children! Today I call you to pray against Satan in a special way. Satan wants to work more now that you know he is active. Dear children, put on your armor against Satan; with Rosaries in your hands you will conquer. Thank you for your response to my call.''

August 15, 1985 (Feast of the Assumption): ''Dear children! Today I bless you, and I want to tell you that I love you. I appeal to you in this moment to live my messages. Today I bless you with a solemn blessing that the Almighty grants me to give. Thank you for your response to my call.''

August 22, 1985: ''Dear children! I call you to prayer especially now when Satan wants to make use of the grapes of your vineyards. Pray that he does not succeed. Thank you for your response to my call.''

September 5, 1985: ''Dear children! Today I thank you for all your prayers. Keep on praying so that Satan will stay far away from this place. Dear children, the plan of Satan has failed. Pray that everything God plans for this village becomes reality. In a special way I want to thank the young people for all the sacrifices they have offered. Thank you for your response to my call.''

September 12, 1985: ''Dear children! I want to ask you that in these days you put the cross in the center. Pray in a special way before the cross; many graces come from the cross. Make a special consecration to the holy cross in your homes. Promise that you will not offend Jesus nor offend against the cross, and that you will not blaspheme. Thank you for your response to my call.''

September 19, 1985: ''Dear children! Today I ask you to live in humility all the message I give you. Dear children, do not become proud living the messages, saying in your hearts, 'I live the messages!' If you bear the messages in your heart and if you live them, then everyone will feel it and there will be no need for words; words are used only by those who do not listen. It is not necessary for you to speak with words. For you, dear children, it is necessary only to live the message and to witness with your lives. Thank you for your response to my call.''

September 26, 1985: ''Dear children! I thank you for all your prayers. Thank you for all the sacrifices. I wish to tell you, dear children, to renew living the messages that I have given you. In particular, live the messages regarding fasting, because your fasting gives me joy. And so you will attain the fulfillment of all the plans that God has for you here in Medjugorje. Thank you for your response to my call.''

October 3, 1985: ''Dear children! I ask you to give thanks to God for all the graces that He gives you. Give thanks to God for all the fruits of His grace, and praise Him. Dear children, learn how to give thanks for little things, and then you will be able to give thanks for great things. Thank you for your response to my call.''

October 10, 1985: ''Dear children! Again today, I want to call you to live the messages in the parish. Especially, I want to call the young people of the parish because this parish is beloved to me. Dear children, if you are living the messages, you live the seed of holiness. As a Mother, I want to call all of you to holiness, so that you can give it to others, because you are like mirrors to other people. Thank you for your response to my call.''

October 17, 1985: ''Dear children! Everything has its time. Today I invite you to begin working on your hearts. All the work in the fields is finished. You found the time to clean out the most abandoned places, but you have neglected your hearts. Work hard and clean up every part of your heart with love. Thank you for responding to my call.''

October 24, 1985: ''Dear children! I want to dress you from day to day in holiness, goodness, obedience, and the love of God, so that from day to day you can be more beautiful and better prepared for your Lord. Dear children, listen to my messages and live them. I desire to lead you! Thank you for responding to my call.''

Birthday Apparition of Mirjana Dragicevic, March 18 and 19, 1985

After receiving the tenth secret at the termination of her regular apparitions of Mary on December 25, 1982, Mirjana was promised an annual "birthday apparition" by Mary. The following is Mirjana's account of her 1985 birthday apparition:

> There were a number of people there. We started waiting for her at four o'clock in the afternoon. We were praying for fifteen minutes, and then she spent fifteen minutes with us. She greeted me like always: "Praised be Jesus" and I responded. She congratulated me on my birthday and then we started our conversation. First she complained because of unbelievers. She said this: "They are my children and I am suffering because of them, because they do not know what is awaiting them if they do not convert to God. Therefore, Mirjana, pray for them!"
>
> Then all of us together prayed. She started two Our Fathers and two Glory Be's to the Father for unbelievers. Then she complained about the greed in the world and in Medjugorje as well. She said: "Woe to those who would take everything from those who are coming (to honour her), and blessed are those from whom they are taking." Then we also prayed for that two Our Fathers and two Glory Be's to the Father.
>
> I asked her that all of us pray for her "Hail Mary" and she smiled at that.
>
> Then we talked about the secrets. I said to her that I have many questions (around thirty) for her. She smiled and said to me not to worry about those, because when I come to answer them I will know all the answers, and she will give me that grace. Otherwise that would take us too much time.
>
> Then I asked about Ivan. She said that the priests should stay with us to help us, because a heavy burden she has put on us and that the suspiciousness of the priests hurt her.
>
> Then I prayed the "Hail Holy Queen!"
>
> Oh, I forgot something. When she was blessing all the holy objects and when she blessed them and when I put all next to me, she asked me to give her the Rosary. Then she took it and starting praying on it and she said: "It is this way to pray on it, tell that to everyone!" She said that the Rosary is not supposed to stay as a decoration, something many have it for. On March 19, she appeared also. The vision lasted seven minutes. There were four of us. We talked about the secrets and we prayed. Nothing else important has happened. On both days she blessed us.

Messages from Jelena Vasilj, the "Seventh Visionary"

Up to March, 1985, Jelena reported to receive messages from Mary by means of inner locutions, seeing and hearing Mary "with her heart". Marijana Vasilj, close friend and common prayer partner with Jelena, also reported experiencing inner locutions from Mary, but the nature of her messages were principally for her own personal spiritual direction.

As of April, 1985, both Jelena and Marijana have begun to receive *external* apparitions of Mary, similar to the three dimensional manner in which the other visionaries receive their apparitions of the Blessed Virgin. The following is a message transmitted by Jelena in April, 1985:

Jelena: You are beautiful.
Mary: I am beautiful because I love. If you want to become
            beautiful, love!

Last Regular Apparition of Ivanka Ivankovic, May 7, 1985

On May 6, 1985, Ivanka received an apparition lasting six minutes longer than the other visionaries present, during which Mary revealed to Ivanka the tenth secret and completed her revelations to Ivanka concerning the future of the world. Mary then asked Ivanka to wait for her alone on the following day for her daily apparitions.

On May 7, Ivanka reported an apparition at her home lasting approximately one hour, which would constitute her last regular apparition of Mary. The following is Ivanka's account of this last regular apparition:

As on every other day Our Lady came with the greeting, "Praised be Jesus Christ". I responded, "May Jesus and Mary always be praised."

I never saw Mary so beautiful as this evening. She was so beautiful and gentle. Today she wore the most beautiful gown I had ever seen in my life. Her gown and also her veil and crown had gold and silver sequins of lights. There were two angels with her. They had the same clothes as Our Lady. The angels were so beautiful. I don't have the words to describe it. One can only experience it.

Our Lady asked me what I would like. Then I asked to see my earthly mother. Our Lady smiled and nodded her head, and at once my mother appeared, she was smiling. Our Lady said to me to stand up. I stood up, my mother embraced me and kissed me and she said, "My child, I am so proud of you." She kissed me and disappeared. After that Our Lady said to me: "My dear child. Today is our last meeting. Do not be sad because I will be coming to you on every anniversary [June 25] except this year. Dear child, do not think that you have done anything wrong, or that this is the reason I will not be coming to you. No, you did not. With all your heart you have accepted the plan which my Son and I had, and you have done everything. No one on this earth has had the grace which you and your brothers and sisters had. Be happy because I am your Mother who loves you with my whole heart.

"Ivanka! Thank you for your response to the call of my Son, and for persevering and for always remaining with Him as long as He asked you. Dear child! Tell all your friends that my Son and myself are always with them, when they ask us and call us. What I have spoken to you these years about the secrets, speak to no one until I tell you."

After this I asked Our Lady if I could kiss her. She nodded her head, and I kissed her. I asked her to bless me, she blessed me, smiled, and said, "Go in God's peace!", and she departed slowly with the two angels.

Thursday Messages Update,
October 31, 1985 to August 21, 1986

October 31, 1985: "Dear children! Today I wish to call you to work in the Church. I do love you equally. I want you to work as much as you can in the Church. I know, dear children, that you can work but you do not want to work because you feel that you are unworthy of the duties. You have to be courageous. With the little flowers you enrich the Church and Jesus so that we can all be happy. Thank you for your response to my call." `

November 7, 1985: "Dear children! I am calling you to love your neighbors, to love those people from whom the evil is coming to you and so, in the power of love, you will be able to judge the intentions of heart. Pray and love, dear children. In the power of love you can do even those things that seem impossible to you. Thank you for your response to my call."

November 14, 1985: "Dear children! I, your mother, love you and I wish to urge you to prayer. I am, dear children, tireless and I call you, even when you are far away from my heart. I feel pain for everyone who has gone astray. But I am a mother and I forgive easily, and I rejoice for every child who comes back to me! Thank you for your response to my call."

November 21, 1985: "Dear children! I wish to tell you that this time is special for you who are from the parish. In the summer you say that you have a lot of work to do. Now there is no work in the fields—work on yourselves personally. Come to the Mass because this time has been given to you. Dear children, there are many of those who come regularly in spite of bad weather because they love me and they wish to show their love in a special way. I ask you to show me your love by coming to the Mass and the Lord will reward you abundantly. Thank you for your response to my call."

November 28, 1985: "Dear children! I want to give thanks to all for all they have done for me, especially the young ones. I beg you, dear children, to come to prayer consciously and in prayer you will know the majesty of God. Thank you for your response to my call."

December 5, 1985: "Dear children! I call you to prepare yourselves for Chistmas by penance, prayer, and works of charity. Don't look at the material, because then you will not be able to experience Christmas. Thank you for your response to my call."

December 12, 1985: "Dear children! For Christmas I invite you to give glory to Jesus together with me. I will give Him to you in a special way on that day, and I invite you on that day to give glory and praise with me to Jesus at His birth. Dear children, pray more on that day and think more about Jesus. Thank you for your response to my call.''

December 19, 1985: ''Dear children! I want to invite you to love your neighbor. If you love your neighbor you will experience Jesus' love more, especially on Christmas day. God will give you a great gift if you abandon yourself to Him. I want to give to mothers, in particular on Christmas day, my maternal blessing and I will bless the others with His blessing. Thank you for your response to my call.''

Wednesday, December 25, 1985 (Christmas Day): Mary appeared with the Baby Jesus.

December 26, 1985: ''Dear children! I want to thank all of you who have listened to my messages and who have lived on Christmas Day what I have told you. I want to guide you. Put aside now from your sins. From now on go forward in love. Abandon your heart to me. Thank you for your response to my call.''

January 2, 1986: ''Dear children! I invite you to decide completely for God. I beg you, dear children, to surrender yourselves completely and you will be able to live everything I say to you. It will not be difficult for you to surrender yourselves completely to God. Thank you for your response to my call.''

January 9, 1986: ''Dear children! I invite you to prayer so that with your prayers you will help Jesus to realize all plans that are here. By offerings and sacrifices to Jesus everything will be fulfilled that is planned. Satan cannot do anything. Thank you for your response to my call.''

January 16, 1986: ''Dear children! I invite you to pray. I need your prayers so much in order that God may be glorified through all of you. Dear children, I beg you to listen and to live your mother's call because I am calling you, by reason of my love, so that I can help you. Thank you for your response to my call.''

January 23, 1986: ''Dear children! Again I invite you to prayer of the heart. If you pray from your heart, dear children, the ice cold hearts of your brothers will be melted and every barrier will disappear. Conversion will be easily achieved by those who want it. You must intercede for this gift for your neighbors. Thank you for your response to my call.''

January 30, 1986: ''Dear children! Today I invite all of you to pray in order that God's plan with you and all that God wills through you may be realized. Help others to be converted, especially those who are coming to Medjugorje. Dear children, do not allow Satan to reign in your hearts. Do not be an image of Satan, but be my image. I am calling you to pray so that you may be witnesses of my presence. God cannot fulfill His will without you. God gave everyone free will and it is up to you to be disposed. Thank you for your response to my call.''

February 7, 1986: "Dear children! This parish is elected by me and is special. It is different from others and I am giving great graces to all who are praying from their hearts. Dear children, I am giving you my messages first of all for the parish and then for all others. The messages are first of all for you, and then for others who will accept them. You will be responsible to me and to my Son Jesus. Thank you for your response to my call."

February 13, 1986: "Dear children! This Lent is a special incentive for you to change. Start from this moment. Turn off the television and renounce other things which are useless. Dear children, I am calling you individually to convert. This time is for you. Thank you for your response to my call."

February 20, 1986: "Dear children! The second message for Lenten Days is that you renew your prayer before the cross. Dear children, I am giving you special graces and Jesus is giving you special gifts from the cross. Accept them and live them. Reflect on Jesus' passion and unite yourselves to Jesus in life. Thank you for your response to my call."

February 27, 1986: "Dear children! Be humble, live in humility. Thank you for your response to my call."

March 6, 1986: Dear children! Today I am calling you to open yourselves more to God so that He can work through you. For as much as you open yourselves you will receive the fruits from it. I wish to call you again to prayer. Thank you for your response to my call."

March 13, 1986: Dear children! Today I am calling you to live this Lent with your little sacrifices. Thank you for every sacrifice you have brought me. Dear children, live in such a way continuously and with love. Help me to bring offerings of your sacrifices to God for which He will reward you. Thank you for your response to my call."

March 20, 1986: Dear children! I am calling you to an active approach to prayer. You wish to live everything I am telling you, but you do not have results from your efforts because you do not pray. Dear children, I beg you to open yourselves and begin to pray. Prayer will be joy. If you begin, it will not be boring because you will pray out of pure joy. Thank you for your response to my call."

March 27, 1986: Dear children! I wish to thank you for your sacrifices and I invite you to the greatest sacrifice, the sacrifice of love. Without love you are not able to accept me or my son. Without love you cannot witness your experience to others. That is why I invite you, dear children, to begin to live the love in your hearts. Thank you for your response to my call."

April 3, 1986: Dear children! I wish to call you to live the Holy Mass. There are many of you who have experienced the beauty of the Mass but there are some who come unwillingly. I have chosen you, dear children, and Jesus is giving you His grace in the Holy Mass. Therefore, consciously live the Holy Mass. Let every coming to Holy Mass be joyful. Come with love and accept the Holy Mass. Thank you for your response to my call."

April 10, 1986: Dear children! I wish to call you to grow in love. A flower cannot grow without water. Neither can you grow without God's blessings. You should pray for blessings from day to day so that you can grow up normally and carry out your activities with God. Thank you for your response to my call."

April 17, 1986: Dear children! Now you are preoccupied about material things and in the material you lose everything that God wants to give you. I am inviting you, dear children, to pray for the gifts of the Holy Spirit that you need now, in order that you may witness my presence here and in everything I am giving you. Dear children, abandon yourselves to me so that I can lead you totally. Do not be so preoccupied about the material things of this world. Thank you for your response to my call."

April 24, 1986: Dear children! Today I am calling you to prayer. You are forgetting that everyone is important, especially the elderly in the family. Incite them to pray. Let all the youth be an example by their lives and testify for Jesus. Dear children, I beg you to start transforming yourselves through prayer and then you will know what you have to do. Thank you for your response to my call."

May 1, 1986: Dear children! I ask you to begin to change your life in your families. Let your family be an harmonious flower which I wish to give to Jesus. Dear children, every family should be active in prayer. It is my wish that the fruits of prayer will be seen one day in the family. Only in that way will I give you as petals to Jesus in fulfillment of God's plan. Thank you for your response to my call."

May 8, 1986: Dear children! You are responsible for the messages. The source of the grace is here, but you, dear children, are the vehicles transmitting the gifts. Therefore, dear children, I am calling you to work responsibly. Everyone will be responsible according to his own measure. Dear children, I am calling you to give the gift to others with love and not to keep it for yourselves. Thank you for your response to my call."

May 15, 1986: Dear children! Today, I am calling you to give me your heart so I can change it to be like mine. You are asking yourselves, dear children, why you cannot respond to what I am seeking from you. You cannot because you have not given me your heart so I can change it. You are seeking, but not acting. I call you to do everything I tell you. In that way I will be with you. Thank you for your response to my call."

May 22, 1986: Dear children! Today I will give you my love. You don't know, dear children, how great is my love and you don't know how to accept it. In many ways I wish to express it but you, dear children, do not recognize it. You don't comprehend my words by your heart and so you are not able to comprehend my love. Dear children, accept me in your life and so you will be able to accept all I am saying to you and all I am calling for you. Thank you for your response to my call.''

May 29, 1986: Dear children! Today I am calling you to a life of love towards God and your neighbor. Without love, dear children, you cannot do anything. Therefore, dear children, I am calling you to live in mutual love. Only in that way can you love me and accept everyone around you. Through coming to your parish, everyone will feel my love through you. Therefore, today I beg you to start with the burning love with which I love you. Thank you for your response to my call.''

June 5, 1986: Dear children! Today I am calling you to decide if you wish to live the messages I am giving you. I wish you to be active in living and transmitting the messages. Especially, dear children, I desire you to be the reflections of Jesus who enlightens an unfaithful world which is walking in darkness. I wish that all of you may be a light to all and witness to the light. Dear children, you are not called to darkness, you are called to light and to live the light in your lives. Thank you for your response to my call.''

June 12, 1986: Dear children! Today I am begging you to pray the rosary with lively faith. Only this way can I help you. Pray. I cannot help you because you don't want to be moved. Dear children, I am calling you to pray the rosary. The rosary should be your commitment, prayed by you with joy and so you will understand why I am visiting you for such a long time. I want to teach you to pray. Thank you for your response to my call.''

June 19, 1986: Dear children! In these days the Lord has allowed me to intercede for more graces for you. Therefore, dear children, I want to urge you once again to pray. Therefore, dear children, I want to urge you once again to pray. Pray constantly and in this way I will give you the joy which the Lord gives me. With these graces, dear children, I want your sufferings to be for you a joy. I am your mother, and I want to help you. Thank you for your response to my call.''

June 24-25, 1986 (the Anniversary): On the anniversary Mary said that she was giving special blessings to all who had come and to all who were associated with Medjugorje. On the evening of the 24th, Mary appeared on the mountaintop to Maria and Ivan, where a group of people had gathered. Maria said she recommended everyone to the Madonna. The Virgin blessed everyone and said, ''Continue to pray here. Pray the rosary again.'' She [Mary] said that this Tabor is for everyone and that we should bring this Tabor experience to all our homes. With this Tabor we must bring peace and reconciliation. Maria said that Mary appeared with five angels and that she was very happy.

June 26, 1986: Dear children! God allowed me to bring about this oasis of peace. I want to invite you to guard it and let the oasis remain pure always. There are those who are destroying peace and prayer by their carelessness. I am calling you to witness and by your life, preserve peace. Thank you for your response to my call.''

July 3, 1986: Dear children! Today I am calling you to prayer. Without prayer you cannot feel me, nor God, nor the grace I am giving you. Therefore, I call you always to begin and end each day with prayer. Dear children, I wish to lead you evermore in prayer, but you cannot grow because you don't want it. I invite you to let prayer have the first place. Thank you for your response to my call.''

July 10, 1986: Dear children! Today I invite you to holiness. You cannot live without holiness. Consequently, overcome all sin with love. Overcome every difficulty you meet with love. Dear children, I beg you to live love within yourselves. Thank you for your response to my call.''

July 17, 1986: Dear children! Today I invite you to meditate on why I am with you for such a long time. I am the mediator between you and God. For that reason, I would like to invite you to live always, out of love, what God is expecting from you. Dear children, live all the messages that I give you in complete humility. Thank you for your response to my call.''

July 24, 1986: Dear children! I am happy about all of you who are on the *way* of holiness, and I am begging you to help all those with your witness who don't know how to live in the way of holiness. For that reason, dear children, your families should be the place where holiness is born. Help everybody to live in a sanctified way, especially your own family. Thank you for your response to my call.''

July 31, 1986: Dear children! Hatred creates division and does not see anybody or anything. I invite you always to carry unity and peace. Especially, dear children, act with love in the place where you live. Let love always be your only tool. With love turn everything to good that the devil wants to destroy and take to himself. Only this way will you be completely mine and I will be able to help you. Thank you for your response to my call.''

August 7, 1986: Dear children! You know I promised an oasis of peace here, but you are not aware that around every oasis is a desert where Satan is lurking. He wants to tempt each one of you. Dear children, only by prayer are you able to overcome every influence of Satan in your place. I am with you, but I can't take away your free will. Thank you for your response to my call.''

August 14, 1986: Dear children! I am inviting you so that your prayer may be a joyful encounter with the Lord. I cannot guide you unless you yourself experience joy in prayer. I want to guide you in prayer more and more, from day to day, but I do not want to force you. Thank you for your response to my call.''

August 21, 1986: Dear children! I am grateful for the love you are showing me. Dear children, you know that I am loving you without limit and that I am praying daily to the Lord so that He may help you to understand the love I am showing you. Therefore, dear children, pray and pray and pray. Thank you for your response to my call.''

BIBLIOGRAPHY

Aquinas, St. Thomas, *Summa Theologiae*. 5 vols., Westminister, Maryland: reprinted by Christian Classics, Inc., 1983.

Aumann, Jordan, O.P., Mulhern, Philip O.P., and O'Donnell, Timothy, *Devotion to the Heart of Jesus*. Rome: Pontifical University of St. Thomas Aquinas, Institute of Spirituality, 1982.

_____, *History of Spirituality*. Manila: St. Paul Publications, 1979.

_____, *Spiritual Theology*. London: Sheed and Ward, 1982.

Bouyer, Rev. Louis, *The Spirituality of the New Testament and the Fathers*. New York: Seabury Press, 1982.

Carol, Juniper B., O.F.M., *Fundamentals of Mariology*. New York: Benzinger Brothers, Inc., 1956.

_____, ed., *Mariology*, 3 Vols., Milwaukee: Bruce Publishing Co., 1954.

Catholic Biblical Association of America, ed. and tr., *The New American Bible*. Boston: Daughters of St. Paul, 1976.

Catholic Biblical Association of Great Britain, ed., *Holy Bible: Revised Standard Version: Catholic Edition*. London Truth Society, 1966.

Coxe, Cleveland, American, ed., *The Anti-Nicene Fathers*, vol. 1. Michigan: reprinted by Eerdmans Publishing Co., 1973.

De Caussade, John-Pierre, *Abandonment to Divine Providence*, John Beevers, trans. New York: Image Books, 1975.

Estrade, Jean-Pierre, *The Appearance of the Blessed Virgin Mary at the Grotto of Lourdes*, J. Girolestrone, trans. Westminster: Art and Book Co., 1912.

Flannery, Austin, O.P., General Editor, *Vatican Council II: The Conciliar and Post-Conciliar Documents*. New York: Costello Publishing Co., 1975.

Flannery, Austin, O.P., General Editor, *Vatican II: More Post-Conciliar Documents*, Vol II. Michigan: Eerdmans Publishing Co., 1982.

Fox, Rev. Robert J., *Fatima Today*. Virginia: Christendom Publications, 1983.

Fuller, Rev. Reginald C., General Editor, *A New Catholic Commentary on Holy Scripture*. Westminster: Thomas Nelson and Sons, Ltd., 1981.

Garrigou-La Grange, Reginald, O.P., *Providence*. Illinois, St. Louis: Herder and Herder Book Co., 1941.

_____, *The Mother of the Saviour and Our Interior Life*, Bernard J. Kelly, C.S.S.P., trans. Dublin: Golden Eagle Books, Ltd., 1948.

Glimm, Francis X., *The Fathers of the Church*, Vol, 1. New York: C.I.M.A. Publishing Co., 1947.

Goodspeed, A., *The Apostolic Fathers*. New York: Harper and Brothers, 1950.

Haffert, John M., *Russia Will Be Converted*. Washington, New Jersey: A.M.I. Press, 1956.

Harden, John, S.J., *The Catholic Catechism*. New York: Doubleday and Company, 1974.

Heim, Ralph, *A Harmony of the Gospels: Revised Standard Version*. Philadelphia: Fortress Press, 1947.

John Paul II, Encyclical Letter, *Dives in Misericordia*. Vatican City: Vatican Polyglot Press, 1980.

_____, Apostolic Exhortation, *Familiaris Consortio*. Vatican City: Vatican Polyglot Press, 1981.

_____, Apostolic Exhortation, *Reconciliatio et Paenitentia*. Vatican City: Vatican Polyglot Press, 1984.

_____, Encyclical Letter, *Redemptor Hominis* Vatican City: Vatican Polyglot Press, 1979.

_____, Apostolic Letter, *Salvific Doloris*. Vatican City: Vatican Polyglot Press, 1984.

Johnston, Francis, *Fatima: The Great Sign*. United Kingdom: Augustine Publishing Co., 1980.

Kleist, James A., S.J., tr., *Ancient Christian Writers*, Vols. 1, 6. Maryland: Newman Press, 1961.

Kondor, Louis, S.V.D., ech., *Fatima in Lucia's Own Words: Sister Lucia's Memoirs*. Fatima: Postulation Center. Distributed by Our Blessed Lady of Victory Mission, Inc., Brookings, South Dakota, 1976.

Kraljevic, Svetozar, O.F.M., *Apparitions of Our Lady of Medjugorje*. Original English manuscript (later edited by Michael Scanlan, T.O.R. and published by Franciscan Herald Press, Chicago, 1984).

Lake, Kirsopp, tr., *The Apostolic Fathers*, 2 Vols. Cambridge: Harvard University Press, 1977.

Lassere, Henry, *Our Lady of Lourdes*, Rev. F. Ignatius Sisk, O.D., trans. London: Burns and Oates, 1875.

Laurentin, René, *Dernieres Nouvelles*, O.E.I.L., ed. France, 1984.

_____, *Documents Authentiques*, 6 Vols. France: P. Lethielleux, 1957.

_____, and Rupcic, Ljudevit, *Is the Virgin Mary Appearing at Medjugorje?*, Francis Martin, trans. Washington, D.C.: The Word Among Us Press, 1984.

Lawson, John, *A Theological and Historical Introduction to the Apostolic Fathers*. New York: Macmillan Co., 1961.

McGinnity, Rev. Gerald, *Medjugorje*. Original manuscipt. Rome: Irish Pontifical College, 1984.

Messages from Jelena Vasilj. Obtained from the St. James Parish Rectory, Medjugorje, Yugoslavia, 1984.

Metzer, Bruce and Isobel, ed., *The Oxford Concise Concordance to the Revised Standard Version of the Holy Bible*. New York: Oxford University Press, 1971.

Neame, Alan, *The Happenings at Lourdes*. London: Catholic Book Club, 1968.

Newman, John Henry, *The Mystical Rose*. London: St. Paul Publications, 1960.

O'Carroll, Michael, C.S. sp., *Theotokos: A Theological Encyclopedia of the Blessed Virgin Mary*. Delaware: Michael Glazier, Inc., 1982.

Ott, Ludwig, *Fundamentals of Catholic Dogma*, Patrick Lynch, trans. Reprinted by Tan Books and Publishers, Rockford, Illinois, 1974.

Paul VI, Apostolic Exhortation, *Marialis Cultus*. London: Catholic Truth Society, 1974.

Pelletier, Joseph, A.A., *Exciting Fatima News: Recently Revealed in Sister Lucia's Letters*. Massachusetts: Assumption Publications, 1975.

_____, *The Immaculate Heart of Mary*. Massachusetts: Assumption Publications, 1976.

_____, *The Sun Danced at Fatima*. Massachusetts: Assumption Publications, 1951.

Quasten, Johannes, *Patrology*, 3 Vols. Maryland: Reprinted by Christian Classics, Inc., 1983.

Recent Messages. Obtained from St. James Parish Rectory, Medjugorje, Yugoslavia, 1985.

Rooney, Lucy, S.N.D. and Robert Faricy, S.J., *Mary, Queen of Peace*. Great Britain: Fowler Wright Books, Ltd., 1984.

Thursday Messages to the Parish of Medjugorje. Obtained from the St. James Parish Rectory, Medjugorje, Yugoslavia, 1984.

Verheylezoon, Louis, S.J., *Devotion to the Sacred Heart of Jesus: Objects, Ends, Practices, Motives*. Reprinted by Tan Books and Publishers, Rockford, Illinois, 1978.

Vlasic, Tomislav, O.F.M., *Our Lady Queen of Peace*. Pamphlet published by Peter Batty, East Sussex, England, 1984.

_____, *Report Sent to Rome by the Parish of Medjugorje*. Obtained from the St. James Parish Rectory, Medjugorje, Yugoslavia, 1984.

Wakefield, Gordon, ed., *A Dictionary of Christian Spirituality*. London: S.C.M. Press, Ltd., 1983.

Walsh, William Thomas, *Our Lady of Fatima*. New York: Image Books, 1954.